CONTENTS

SCOPE AND SEQUENCE

UNIT	WATCH AND LISTEN	LISTENINGS	LISTENING SKILLS	PRONUNCIATION FOR LISTENING	
1 GLOBALIZATION *Academic Disciplines* Cultural Studies / Sociology	NBA Fans in China	1: A radio program about the global food industry 2: A presentation about energy use in food production	*Key Skill* Activating prior knowledge *Additional Skills* Understanding key vocabulary Using your knowledge Listening for main ideas Listening for details Listening for opinion Understanding cause and effect Taking notes Synthesizing	Consonant clusters	
2 EDUCATION *Academic Disciplines* Communications / Education	A Soybean-Powered Car	1: A meeting between a student and an academic advisor 2: A conversation between students about paths towards a medical profession	*Key Skills* Listening for advice and suggestions Making inferences *Additional Skills* Understanding key vocabulary Using your knowledge Listening for main ideas Listening for details Listening for opinion Taking notes Synthesizing	Certain and uncertain intonation	
3 MEDICINE *Academic Disciplines* Health Sciences / Medicine	Corporate Wellness	1: A college seminar about pandemics 2: A debate about flu vaccines	*Key Skills* Identifying contrasting opinions Strengthening points in an argument *Additional Skills* Understanding key vocabulary Using your knowledge Listening for main ideas Listening for opinion Listening for attitude Listening for details Taking notes Synthesizing	Intonation in tag questions	
4 THE ENVIRONMENT *Academic Disciplines* Ecology / Environmental Studies	Cloning Endangered Species	1: A lecture about habitat destruction 2: A talk about the decline of desert habitats	*Key Skills* Distinguishing main ideas from details Taking notes on main ideas and details *Additional Skills* Understanding key vocabulary Using your knowledge Listening for main ideas Listening for details Listening for opinion Listening for text organization Summarizing Taking notes Synthesizing	Sentence stress	

LISTENING AND SPEAKING 3

TEACHER'S MANUAL

Lewis Lansford

Robyn Brinks Lockwood

with
Christina Cavage
Angela Blackwell
Jeanne Lambert
Janet Gokay

CAMBRIDGE
UNIVERSITY PRESS

CAMBRIDGE
UNIVERSITY PRESS

University Printing House, Cambridge CB2 8BS, United Kingdom

One Liberty Plaza, 20th Floor, New York, NY 10006 USA

477 Williamstown Road, Port Melbourne, VIC 3207 Australia

4843/24, 2nd Floor, Ansari Road, Daryaganj, Delhi – 110002, India

79 Anson Road, #06–04/06, Singapore 079906

Cambridge University Press is part of the University of Cambridge.

It furthers the University's mission by disseminating knowledge in the pursuit of education, learning and research at the highest international levels of excellence.

www.cambridge.org
Information on this title: www.cambridge.org/9781316625408

First published 2017

20 19 18 17 16 15 14 13 12 11 10 9 8 7 6 5 4 3 2 1

Printed in Malaysia by Vivar Printing

A catalogue record for this publication is available from the British Library

ISBN 978-1-316-62540-8 Teacher's Manual 3 Listening and Speaking
ISBN 978-1-316-62099-1 Student's Book with Online Workbook 3 Listening and Speaking

	LANGUAGE DEVELOPMENT	CRITICAL THINKING	SPEAKING	ON CAMPUS
	Modals of present and past probability Globalization and environment vocabulary	Understanding, analyzing, and using data in pie charts	*Speaking Skills* Presenting data Describing a pie chart Drawing conclusions from data *Speaking Task* Give a presentation using data from a pie chart on how we can ensure that workers in developing countries are paid fairly for the food we import.	*Presentation Skill* Involving the audience
	Stating preferences with *would*	Prioritizing criteria Using priorities to evaluate options	*Speaking Skills* Giving an opinion and making suggestions Agreeing and disagreeing respectfully Compromising and finalizing a decision *Pronunciation* Certain and uncertain intonation *Speaking Task* Decide as a group which candidate should receive a scholarship.	*Communication Skill* Being an active listener
	Health science vocabulary Conditionals: • Past unreal conditionals • Present and future unreal conditionals	Understanding background and motivation	*Speaking Skill* Using persuasive language *Speaking Task* Role-play a debate between representatives from an international aid organization and representatives from a drug company.	*Presentation Skill* Citing sources in a presentation
	Multi-word prepositions The past perfect Verbs to describe environmental change	Organizing information in a presentation	*Speaking Skills* Giving background information Signposting *Speaking Task* Give a presentation about a change in the environment and discuss possible solutions.	*Study Skill* Time management

UNIT	WATCH AND LISTEN	LISTENINGS	LISTENING SKILLS	PRONUNCIATION FOR LISTENING	
5 ARCHITECTURE *Academic Disciplines* Architecture / Urban Planning	The Skyscraper	1: A conversation between two property developers 2: A housing development meeting	*Key Skills* Understanding figurative language Understanding strong and tentative suggestions *Additional Skills* Understanding key vocabulary Using your knowledge Listening for main ideas Listening for details Listening for attitude Taking notes Synthesizing	Emphasis in contrasting opinions	
6 ENERGY *Academic Disciplines* Engineering / Physics	Solar Panels at Home	1: A radio show about the island of El Hierro, Spain 2: A chaired meeting about saving energy in an office	*Key Skills* Understanding digressions Understanding persuasive techniques *Additional Skills* Understanding key vocabulary Using your knowledge Listening for main ideas Listening for details Listening for text organization Taking notes Synthesizing	Intonation related to emotion	
7 ART AND DESIGN *Academic Disciplines* Design / Fine Art	Jen Lewin's Light and Sound Installations	1: A radio report about graffiti 2: An informal debate about public art	*Key Skills* Inferring opinions Distinguishing fact from opinion *Additional Skills* Understanding key vocabulary Predicting content using visuals Using your knowledge Listening for main ideas Listening for details Listening for opinion Making inferences Taking notes Synthesizing	Stress in word families	
8 AGING *Academic Disciplines* Economics / Sociology	Baby Boomers' Retirement Style	1: A finance podcast 2: Two student presentations on aging in different countries	*Key Skill* Understanding specific observations and generalizations *Additional Skills* Understanding key vocabulary Using your knowledge Listening for main ideas Listening for details Taking notes Synthesizing	Consonant reductions and joined vowels	

LANGUAGE DEVELOPMENT	CRITICAL THINKING	SPEAKING	ON CAMPUS
Future forms: • *Will* and *be going to* for predictions and expectations Academic vocabulary for architecture and transformation	Analyzing and evaluating requirements for solutions	*Speaking Skills* Identifying problems and suggesting solutions: • Presenting a problem • Making polite suggestions • Responding to suggested solutions *Pronunciation* Emphasizing a word or idea to signal a problem *Speaking Task* Discuss a housing problem and possible solutions.	*Life Skill* Understanding college expectations
Connecting ideas between sentences: • Transition words and phrases The passive voice Academic vocabulary for networks and systems	Identifying, analyzing, and evaluating problems and solutions	*Speaking Skills* Keeping a discussion moving: • Asking for input, summarizing, and keeping a discussion moving • Dealing with interruptions and digressions *Pronunciation* Using a neutral tone of voice *Speaking Task* Participate in a discussion about an energy problem and suggest possible solutions.	*Communication Skill* Working in groups
Relative clauses: • Identifying and nonidentifying relative clauses	Debate statements and responses Taking notes for a debate Evaluating reasons Analyzing evidence	*Speaking Skills* Language for debates: • Expressing contrasting opinions • Restating somebody's point • Language for hedging *Pronunciation* Stress in hedging language *Speaking Task* Have an informal debate about whether or not public money should be spent on public art.	*Life Skill* Choosing a major
Verbs with infinitives or gerunds	Understanding, analyzing, and evaluating data from a line graph	*Speaking Skills* Referencing data in a presentation: • Explaining details and trends in a graph • Explaining causes and effects *Pronunciation* Contrastive stress in numbers and comparisons *Speaking Task* Give a presentation using graphical data on how aging has changed a country's population over time and the impact this is likely to have on its society in the future.	*Life Skill* The world of work

***Prism* is a five-level paired skills series for beginner- to advanced-level students of North American English.** Its five Listening and Speaking and five Reading and Writing levels are designed to equip students with the language and skills to be successful both inside and outside of the college classroom.

***Prism* uses a fresh approach to Critical Thinking based on a full integration of Bloom's taxonomy to help students become well-rounded critical thinkers.** The productive half of each unit begins with Critical Thinking. This section gives students the skills and tools they need to plan and prepare for success in their Speaking or Writing Task. Learners develop lower- and higher-order thinking skills, ranging from demonstrating knowledge and understanding to in-depth evaluation and analysis of content. Margin labels in the Critical Thinking sections highlight exercises that develop Bloom's concepts.

***Prism* focuses on the most relevant and important language for students of academic English based on comprehensive research.** Key vocabulary is taken from the General Service List, the Academic Word List, and the Cambridge English Corpus. The grammar selected is also corpus-informed.

***Prism* goes beyond language and critical thinking skills to teach students how to be successful, engaged college students both inside and outside of the classroom.** On Campus spreads at the end of each unit introduce students to communication, study, presentation, and life skills that will help them transition to life in North American community college and university programs.

***Prism* combines print and digital solutions for the modern student and program.** Online workbooks give students additional graded language and skills practice. Audio and video resources are available to students and teachers in the same platform. Presentation Plus gives teachers modern tools to enhance their students' learning environment in the classroom.

***Prism* provides assessment resources for the busy teacher.** Photocopiable unit quizzes and answer keys are included in the Teacher's Manual, with downloadable PDF and Word versions available at Cambridge.org/prism and in the Resource tab of the Cambridge Learning Management System. Speaking rubrics for grading Speaking Tasks are included in the Teacher's Manual.

SERIES LEVELS

Level	Description	CEFR Levels
Prism Intro	Beginner	A1
Prism 1	Low Intermediate	A2
Prism 2	Intermediate	B1
Prism 3	High Intermediate	B2
Prism 4	Advanced	C1

UNIT OPENER

Each unit opens with a striking two-page photo related to the topic, a Learning Objectives box, and an Activate Your Knowledge activity.

PURPOSE

- To introduce and generate interest in the unit topic with an engaging visual
- To set the learning objectives for the unit
- To make connections between students' background knowledge and the unit topic/theme

TEACHING SUGGESTIONS
PHOTO SPREAD

Lead an open class discussion on the connection between the unit opener photo and topic. Start off with questions like:
- *What is the first thing you notice in the photographs?*
- *What do you think of when you look at the photo?*
- *How is the photo connected to the unit title?*

ACTIVATE YOUR KNOWLEDGE

After students work in pairs to answer the questions, have volunteers share with the class answers to questions that generated the most discussion.

You can also use the exercise to practice fluency. Instruct students to answer the questions as quickly as possible without worrying about creating grammatically correct sentences. Keep time and do not allow students more than 15–60 seconds per answer, depending on level and complexity of the question. You can then focus on accuracy when volunteers share their answers with the class.

WATCH AND LISTEN

Each unit includes a short authentic video from a respected news source that is related to the unit topic, along with exercises for students to do before, during, and after watching. The video can be played in the classroom or watched outside of class by students via the Cambridge LMS.

Note: A glossary defines above-level or specialized words that appear in the video so that teachers do not have to spend time pre-teaching or explaining this vocabulary while viewing.

PURPOSE

- To create a varied and dynamic learning experience
- To generate further interest in and discussion of the unit topic
- To build background knowledge and ideas on the topic
- To develop and practice key skills in prediction, comprehension, and discussion
- To personalize and give opinions on a topic

TEACHING SUGGESTIONS
PREPARING TO WATCH

Have students work in pairs to complete the Activating Your Knowledge exercise. Then have volunteers share their answers. Alternately, students can complete this section on their own, and then compare answers with a partner.

For a livelier class discussion, look at the visuals from the Predicting Content Using Visuals exercise as a class and answer the questions together.

WHILE WATCHING

Watch the video twice, once while students listen for main ideas and once while they listen for key details. After each viewing, facilitate a discussion of students' answers and clarify any confusion. If some students still have trouble with comprehension, suggest that they watch the video again at home or during a computer lab session.

DISCUSSION

Have students work in pairs or small groups to answer the discussion questions. Have students compare their answers with another pair or group. Then have volunteers share their answers with the class. If possible, expand on their answers by making connections between their answers and the video content. For example: *That's an interesting perspective. How is it similar to what the speaker in the video mentioned? How is it different?*

LISTENING

The first half of each unit focuses on the receptive skill of listening. Each unit includes two listening passages that provide different angles, viewpoints, and/or genres related to the unit topic. All audio files are available for student use in the *Prism* online workbook. Audio scripts are provided in the back of the student's book, as well as in the teacher's manual.

LISTENING 1

Listening 1 includes a listening passage on an academic topic. It provides information on the unit topic, and it gives students exposure to and practice with language and listening skills while helping them begin to generate ideas for their final Speaking Task.

PREPARING TO LISTEN

PURPOSE

- To prepare students to understand the content of the listening
- To help students anticipate what they will hear using visuals and prior knowledge
- To introduce and build key academic and topical vocabulary for the listening and for the final Speaking Task

TEACHING SUGGESTIONS

Encourage students to complete the pre-listening activities in this section in pairs or groups. This will promote a high level of engagement. Once students have completed the activities, check for understanding and offer any clarification.

Encourage or assign your students to keep a vocabulary notebook for new words. This should include new key vocabulary words, parts of speech, definitions (in the students' own words), and contextual sentences. To extend the vocabulary activity in this section, ask students to find synonyms, antonyms, or related terms for the vocabulary items they just practiced. These can then be added to their vocabulary notebooks.

Key vocabulary exercises can also be assigned ahead of time so that you can focus on the listening content and skills in class.

WHILE LISTENING

PURPOSE

- To introduce, review, and/or practice key academic listening skills
- To practice listening comprehension and note-taking skills
- To hear key vocabulary in a natural academic context
- To provide information and stimulate ideas on an academic topic

TEACHING SUGGESTIONS

Depending on class level, you can break up the audio into more manageable parts as students complete the exercises. Because students can access the audio files at any time through their online resources, consider having them listen to the passage for homework before class so that they are familiar with the content. This also gives you a chance to check in with your students about the difficulty level of the passage. Students who still struggle with comprehension can listen again for homework.

For more open-ended note-taking practice, have students listen and take notes with books closed. During the first listening, instruct them to take notes on main ideas and general points. Then with your guidance, have them listen again to take notes on specific details. They can then use their notes to complete the exercises in the section.

POST-LISTENING

PURPOSE

- To analyze, expand on, and/or practice key pronunciation or listening skills from the previous section
- To introduce, review, and/or practice key critical thinking skills applied to content from the listening passage

TEACHING SUGGESTIONS

Have students complete the activities in pairs or small groups; do not play the audio again at this point. After checking answers, survey students on what they found most challenging in the section. Then have students listen to the audio again for homework and take additional notes on the challenging skills and content, to be shared at the beginning of the next class or in an online forum.

PRONUNCIATION FOR LISTENING

This section appears in each unit but changes position based on where it most logically belongs.

PURPOSE

- To help students anticipate and understand pronunciation trouble spots while listening to authentic academic discourse

TEACHING SUGGESTIONS

Review the Pronunciation for Listening skills box as a class to ensure that students understand the explanation and examples before doing the exercises.

If possible, assign a podcast, video, Online Workbook listening, or other source for students to listen to and locate instances of the Pronunciation for Listening skill.

DISCUSSION

PURPOSE

- To give students the opportunity to discuss what they heard and offer opinions
- To think critically about what they just heard
- To further personalize the topic and issues in Listening 1

TEACHING SUGGESTIONS

Give students three to five minutes to discuss and jot down notes for their answers. Monitor student groups, taking notes on common mistakes. Then survey the students on their favorite questions and have groups volunteer to share their answers to them. You can provide oral or written feedback on common mistakes at the end of the section.

LANGUAGE DEVELOPMENT

Each unit includes the introduction and practice of academic language relevant to the unit topic and useful for the unit Speaking Task. This may include vocabulary and/or grammar points that appear in one or both of the unit listening passages.

PURPOSE
- To recycle and expand on vocabulary that may appear in Listening 1
- To recycle and expand on grammar that may appear in Listening 1
- To expose students to corpus-informed, research-based language for the unit topic and level
- To practice language and structures that will improve student accuracy and fluency in the final Speaking Task

TEACHING SUGGESTIONS

For grammar points, review the language box as a class and facilitate answers to any unclear sections. Alternatively, have students review it in pairs and allow time for questions. Then have students work in pairs to complete the accompanying activities. Review students' answers and allow time for any clarification.

For vocabulary points, have students complete the exercises in pairs. Then review answers and allow time for any clarification. To extend this activity, have students create sentences using each term and/or make a list of synonyms, antonyms, or related words and phrases for each term. Students should also add relevant language to their vocabulary notebooks. For homework, have students annotate the audio scripts in the back of the book, underlining or highlighting any language covered in this section.

LISTENING 2

Listening 2 is a listening passage on the unit topic but from a different angle and often in a different format than Listening 1. It gives students additional exposure to and practice with language and listening skills while helping them generate and refine ideas for their final Speaking Task.

PREPARING TO LISTEN

PURPOSE
- To prepare students to understand the content of the listening
- To help students anticipate content using visuals and prior knowledge
- To introduce and build key academic and topical vocabulary for the listening and for the final Speaking Task

TEACHING SUGGESTIONS

Encourage students to complete the pre-listening activities in this section in pairs or small groups to promote a high level of engagement. Circulate among students at this time, taking notes of common areas of difficulty. Once students have completed the activities, check for understanding and offer clarification, paying particular attention to any problem areas you noted.

If you wish to extend the vocabulary activity in this section, elicit other word forms of the key vocabulary. Model pronunciation of these word forms so that students are able to recognize them in context.

WHILE LISTENING

PURPOSE

- To introduce, review, and/or practice key academic listening skills
- To practice listening comprehension and note-taking skills
- To hear key vocabulary and Language Development elements in a natural academic context
- To provide information and stimulate ideas on an academic topic
- To model certain aspects or elements of the final Speaking Task

TEACHING SUGGESTIONS

As with Listening 1, you can break up the audio into more manageable parts as students complete the exercises. Depending on time and proficiency level, have students listen to the passage for homework before class so that they are familiar with the content. Check in with them about the difficulty level of the passage in comparison with Listening 1. Assign students who still struggle with comprehension to listen again for homework. Set specific questions for them to answer or areas for them to take notes on.

POST-LISTENING

PURPOSE

- To analyze, expand on, and/or practice key pronunciation or listening skills from the previous section
- To introduce, review, and/or practice key critical thinking skills applied to content from the listening passage

TEACHING SUGGESTIONS

Have students complete the activities in pairs or small groups; do not play the audio again at this point. After checking answers, survey students on what they found most challenging in the section. Then have students listen to the audio again for homework and take additional notes on the challenging skills and content, to be shared at the beginning of the next class or in an online forum.

DISCUSSION

PURPOSE

- To personalize and expand on the ideas and content of Listening 2
- To practice synthesizing the content of the unit listening passages
- To transition students from the receptive to the productive half of the unit

TEACHING SUGGESTIONS

Before students discuss the questions in this section the first time, introduce the key skill of synthesis. Start by defining synthesis (combining and analyzing ideas from multiple sources). Stress its importance in higher education: in college or graduate school, students will be asked to synthesize ideas from a wide range of sources, to think critically about them, to make connections among them, and to add their own ideas. Note: you may need to review this information periodically with your class.

Have students answer the questions in pairs or small groups, and then ask for volunteers to share their answers with the class. Facilitate the discussion, encouraging students to make connections between Listening 1 and Listening 2. If applicable, ask students to relate the content of the unit video to this section. This is also a good context in which to introduce the Speaking Task at the beginning of the next section and to have students consider how the content of the listening passages relates to the prompt.

SPEAKING

The second half of each unit focuses on the productive skill of speaking. It begins with the prompt for the unit Speaking Task and systematically equips students with the skills and language to plan for, prepare, and execute the task successfully.

CRITICAL THINKING

PURPOSE

- To introduce the unit Speaking Task.
- To help generate, develop, and organize ideas for the Speaking Task.
- To teach and practice the lower-order critical thinking skills of remembering, understanding, and applying knowledge through practical brainstorming and organizational activities
- To teach and practice the higher-order critical thinking skills of analyzing, evaluating, and creating in order to prepare students for success in the Speaking Task and, more generally, in the college classroom

TEACHING SUGGESTIONS

Encourage students to work through this section collaboratively in pairs or small groups to promote a high level of engagement. Facilitate their learning and progress by circulating and checking in with students as they work through this section. If time permits, have groups exchange and evaluate one another's work.

PREPARATION FOR SPEAKING

PURPOSE

- To introduce and practice academic speaking skills that can be used in the Speaking Task
- To introduce or recycle language that supports these key skills and the Speaking Task
- To help students ensure correct pronunciation

Note: Some units include a Pronunciation for Speaking skills box and practice in this section.

TEACHING SUGGESTIONS

Review any skills boxes in this section as a class and clarify points of confusion. Then have students work on the activities in pairs or small groups. After they complete any speaking activities, have some students share their answers with the class.

Since the section focuses on form and function, it is important to offer corrective feedback to your students. You can then focus on fluency in the next section. Below are two examples of ways to provide interactive corrective feedback:

1) Student says, "*It possible to use that technology today.*" Teacher writes the incorrect form on the board and asks a student to come to the board and correct the statement.
2) Teacher repeats the incorrect statement orally to see if the student can self-correct. If not, then teacher prompts the student – for example, "*Are you missing a subject/verb/ preposition?*")

In all cases, the correct form should be modeled for the student and for the rest of the class.

SPEAKING TASK

PURPOSE

- To work collaboratively in preparation for the Speaking Task
- To revisit, revise, and expand on work done in the Critical Thinking section
- To provide an opportunity for students to synthesize the language, skills, and ideas presented and generated in the unit
- To improve oral fluency

Depending on time and class level, students can complete the preparation activities for homework or in class. If conducted in class, work should be done collaboratively. It can be helpful to pair a quieter student with a more outgoing student. It is also important to circulate among students, asking and answering questions as needed.

If students agree, record the Speaking Tasks on a phone or video camera. At the same time, take notes on key areas, such as grammar, pronunciation, key word stress, eye contact, and pacing. Students can view their performances and your written feedback at the same time.

ON CAMPUS

Each unit concludes with a unique spread that teaches students concepts and skills that go beyond traditional listening and speaking academic skills.

PURPOSE

- To familiarize students with all aspects of the North American college experience
- To enable students to interact and participate successfully in the college classroom
- To prepare students to navigate a typical North American college campus

TEACHING SUGGESTIONS

PREPARING TO LISTEN

Begin with an open discussion by asking students what they know about the topic. For example:

- *What is culture shock?*
- *Have you ever met with an academic advisor?*
- *How do college students choose a major?*
- *What is active learning?*

You can also write the question on the board and assign as pair work, and have students share their answers with the class.

WHILE LISTENING

Have students listen once and complete the accompanying activities. Have them listen again and check their work. You can extend these activities by asking the following questions:

- *What stood out to you the most in this listening passage?*
- *What did you understand more clearly when you listened the second time?*
- *Which part or speaker had the most impact on you and why?"*

PRACTICE

Have students read any skills boxes silently. Give them two minutes to discuss the information with a partner before they complete the exercises. Elicit from some volunteers how the exercises practice what they heard in the listening passage.

REAL-WORLD APPLICATION

Depending on time, you may want to assign the activities in this section as homework. Having students collaborate on these real-world tasks either inside or outside of the classroom simulates a common practice in college and graduate school. At the beginning of the week you can set up a schedule so that several student groups present their work during class throughout the week.

To extend this section, assign small related research projects, as applicable. For example, have students research and report on three websites with information on choosing a college major.

PRISM SPEAKING TASK RUBRIC

CATEGORY	CRITERIA	SCORE
Pronunciation	• Pronunciation is clear and understandable. • Word/sentence stress and intonation is natural. • Speaker demonstrates mastery of unit pronunciation skills.	
Fluency	• Speech is clear and articulate without long unnatural pauses. • Speaker is able to move the conversation or presentation forward naturally. • Speaker is able to adjust to questions and input from other speakers.	
Content	• Content is appropriate and reflects a good understanding of the topic. • Content is well-organized and easy to follow. • Speaker demonstrates mastery of unit Language Development points.	
Vocabulary	• Vocabulary, including expressions and transition language, is accurate, appropriate, and varied. • Speaker demonstrates mastery of unit key vocabulary.	
Comprehension	• Speaker demonstrates a strong understanding of the speaking prompt and task at hand. • Speaker is able to understand and respond to other speakers accurately and appropriately.	

How well does the response meet the criteria?	Recommended Score
At least 90%	20
At least 75%	15
At least 60%	10
At least 50%	5
Less than 50%	0
Total Score Possible per Section	20
Total Score Possible	100

Feedback:

UNIT 1
ACTIVATE YOUR KNOWLEDGE
page 15
Answers will vary.

WATCH AND LISTEN

Exercise 1 page 16
Answers will vary.

Exercise 2 page 16
Answers will vary.

Exercise 3 page 17
1 T
2 F; The percentage of NBA games viewed by the Chinese population grew by 30% in the previous year.
3 T
4 T

Exercise 4 page 17
1 13,000 people came to a practice in Shanghai.
2 Players toured the Great Wall.
3 Last year the revenue was around $150 million.

Exercise 5 page 17
Answers will vary.

Exercise 6 page 17
Answers will vary.

LISTENING 1

Exercise 1 page 18
a purchase
b overseas
c consumers
d imported
e greenhouse
f produce
g investigate

Exercise 2 page 19
Answers will vary.

Exercise 3 page 19
Topics 1, 2, and 7

Exercise 4 page 19
1 how globalization allows us to taste food from different cultures around the world
2 David Green
3 fruit
4 vegetables
5 eat healthfully
6 Bananas
7 Tomatoes
8 California

9 Costa Rica
10 2,500
11 2,300
12 they need to have fresh fruit in winter
13 increases production costs
14 11,000
15 footprint

Exercise 5 page 20
1 T
2 F; David doesn't really think about where his food comes from.
3 F; The global food industry allows people all over the world to eat a huge variety of fresh fruit and vegetables.
4 F; You can only really be sure how far something has traveled if you purchase it directly from a farm or if you grow it yourself.
5 F; Even something that looks like it's local can have a big impact on the environment.

Exercise 6 page 20
1 a
2 b
3 a

Exercise 7 page 21
1 going
2 tea
3 find
4 sewed
5 timed
6 Flying
7 pass
8 cost

Exercise 8 page 21
1 support
2 three
3 First
4 sixth
5 climate
6 state
7 trap
8 growing
9 would
10 rain

Exercise 9 page 21
Answers will vary.

LANGUAGE DEVELOPMENT

Exercise 1 page 23
1 may have bought
2 must be
3 must have lost
4 might send
5 can't be
6 must have lived

Exercise 2 page 23
1 must be
2 must have been
3 might/may/could contain
4 may have been
5 couldn't/can't have been

Exercise 3 page 24
1 carbon footprint
2 transportation
3 carbon emissions
4 processing
5 climate change
6 supply chain
7 purchasing
8 produce
9 imported

LISTENING 2

Exercise 1 page 25
1 a
2 a
3 b
4 b
5 b
6 a
7 b

Exercise 2 page 25
Answers will vary.

Exercise 3 page 26

main contributor	examples
1 energy used in homes to store and prepare food	– refrigeration – cooking with gas or electrical appliances
2 processing	– putting vegetables in cans – turning ingredients into ready-made meals
3 agriculture	– growing produce in greenhouses

Exercise 4 page 26
1 a
2 d
3 c
4 b

Exercise 5 page 26
households: 29%
wholesale and retail: 14%
processing: 20%
packaging: 6%
transportation: 4%
agriculture: 15%
food service: 12%

Exercise 6 page 27
1 airplanes create pollution that causes environmental problems
2 Experts argue that foods that are the least damaging to the environment are usually the ones grown locally.
3 These greenhouses are heated

Exercise 7 page 27
1 because
2 Consequently
3 therefore

Exercise 8 page 27
Answers will vary.

Exercise 9 page 27
Answers will vary.

Exercise 10 page 27
Answers will vary.

CRITICAL THINKING

Exercise 1 page 28
1 the percentage of profit for each step in the process
2 nine
3 they would increase

Exercise 2 page 29
1 supermarket
2 plantation worker
3 international transportation
4 5%
5 9%

Exercise 3 page 29
1 O
2 S
3 O
4 O

Exercise 4 page 29
Possible answers:
1 the cost of storing, advertising, and paying workers
2 the workers are paid little
3 Plantation owners have to pay for the land and growing supplies, and workers do not.
4 It would grow because the pie must still equal 100%.
5 The price would go up so other sections can make the same amount of money.

Exercise 6 page 30
Answers will vary.

PREPARATION FOR SPEAKING

Exercises 1–2 page 30
1 I'd like to talk about
2 a lot of discussion
3 Many people believe
4 others have pointed out
5 They say
6 would like to show
7 look at
8 consider

Exercise 3 page 31
1 The largest part; a quarter of
2 accounts for
3 each make up; a total of
4 Three parts are related to; they make up

Exercise 4 page 32
1 b
2 f
3 a
4 g
5 c
6 e
7 d

Exercise 5 page 32
1 e
2 a
3 d
4 c
5 b

ON CAMPUS

Exercise 1 page 34
B is more effective because the speaker speaks directly to the audience, asks questions, and waits for a response.

Exercise 3 page 34
1 how much food is wasted in the U.S. every year
2 the financial cost of wasting food
3 the effects on the environment of wasting food
4 global needs for food now and in the future

Exercise 4 page 35
1 begin the story with a dramatic statement
2 ask questions, ask audience to react
3 ask questions
4 refer to audience experience
5 rephrase statistics

Exercise 5 page 35
1 f
2 d
3 c
4 b
5 e
6 a

Exercises 6–7 page 35
Answers will vary.

UNIT 2
ACTIVATE YOUR KNOWLEDGE
page 37
Answers will vary.

WATCH AND LISTEN

Exercise 1 page 38
Answers will vary.

Exercise 2 page 38
Answers will vary.

Exercise 3 page 39
1 T
2 T
3 F; The car was designed and created by high school auto shop students.
4 F; The auto shop class spent one year building the car.
5 T

Exercise 4 page 39
1 attracted
2 hybrid
3 difficulties
4 an opportunity

Exercise 5 page 39
1 c   2 a   3 b

Exercise 6 page 39
Answers will vary.

LISTENING 1
Exercise 1 page 40
Answers will vary.

Exercise 2 page 40
1 internship
2 academic
3 vocational
4 acquire

5 understanding
6 advisor
7 mechanical
8 specialist

Exercise 4 page 41
1 what to major in
2 engineering
3 talk to some engineers and visit an
  engineering company

Exercise 5 page 42
1 math; physics
2 mechanical
3 engineering
4 courses
5 professors; classes
6 career
7 graduates; jobs
8 computer; visit

Exercise 6 page 43
2 C
3 C
4 U
5 C
6 U
7 C
8 U

Exercise 7 page 43

certain	uncertain
1 definitely 2 for sure	3 wonder 4 consider 5 not sure

Exercise 8 page 43
Answers will vary.

LANGUAGE DEVELOPMENT

Exercise 1 page 45
1 take
2 to work
3 participating
4 to stay
5 working
6 see

Exercise 2 page 45
Answers will vary. Possible answers:
1 Would you prefer to work for a lot of money or for
  career satisfaction?
2 I'd rather study for a Master's degree.
3 Would they like to apply to a university in Riyadh?
4 He'd rather consider studying medicine.
5 Would she like to take a theoretical course?
6 I'd rather not start working right away.

LISTENING 2

Exercise 1 page 46
1 medical
2 technical
3 physical
4 manual
5 professional
6 complex
7 secure
8 practical

Exercise 2 page 47
Answers will vary.

Exercise 3 page 48
Answers will vary. Possible answers:

emergency medical technician (EMT)	emergency room nurse
Pros: exciting, takes less time, can become a specialist **Cons:** tough, physical job	**Pros:** pay is better **Cons:** takes more time

Exercise 4 page 48
EMT

Exercise 5 page 48

	medical student	Adam
1	✓	
2		✓
3		✓
4		✓
5		✓
6	✓	
7	✓	
8		✓

Exercise 6 page 49
Possible answers:
1 The medical student probably thinks Adam should do
  the EMT course because he is so enthusiastic about it.
2 Probably helping people, being independent and
  making decisions on his own. He speaks more and
  his tone is more positive when he talks about these
  factors of the EMT job.
For both questions, you can tell by whether the medical
student's and Adam's intonation is rising or falling when
they are discussing different aspects of the two jobs
Adam is considering.

Exercise 7 page 49
Answers will vary.

CRITICAL THINKING
Exercises 1–5 pages 50–52
Answers will vary.

PREPARATION FOR SPEAKING
Exercises 1–2 page 53
1 e
2 d
3 a
4 f
5 c
6 b
1, 2, and 6 give an opinion; 3, 4, and 5 are suggestions.

Exercise 3 page 54
1 D
2 A
3 A
4 D
5 D
6 D
7 A

Exercise 4 page 54
Answers will vary.

Exercises 5–6 page 54
1 understandable
2 point
3 right
4 that
5 decision
6 agreement

Exercise 7 page 54
1 C
2 C
3 U
4 U
5 C
6 U

ON CAMPUS
Exercise 1 page 56
1 T
2 F; Students need to take 120 credit hours to graduate.
3 T
4 F; A three-credit class means approximately three hours of class a week.
5 T
6 T
7 F; To pass a class, you need to get at least a C.
8 T

Exercise 3 page 56
1 say that again
2 ask a question
3 correct
4 other words
5 give us an example
6 ask about grades
7 explain the term GPA

Exercise 4 page 57
1 a
2 c
3 e
4 f
5 b
6 d

Exercise 5 page 57
1 Is that correct
2 Can you give us an example
3 So in other words
4 What's the difference between

Exercises 6–7 page 57
Answers will vary.

UNIT 3
ACTIVATE YOUR KNOWLEDGE
page 59
Answers will vary.

WATCH AND LISTEN
Exercise 1 page 60
Answers will vary.

Exercise 2 page 60
Answers will vary.

Exercise 3 page 61
1 T
2 F; The program benefits employees and the employer.
3 F; Employees in the program are sick less often and are more productive.
4 T
5 F; Corporate wellness programs often have on-site gyms where employees can take a cardio class during their work day.

Exercise 4 page 61
1 She was overweight, suffered from health problems
2 $1,000
3 Company has less claim costs, fewer days out sick, higher productivity from employees, and more engaged employees
4 4,013,800
5 fresh, healthy choices

Exercise 5–6 page 61
Answers will vary.

LISTENING 1

Exercise 1 page 62

a occur
b recover
c contract
d infected
e prevention
f outbreak
g treatment
h factor

Exercises 2–3 page 63

1 people's general health, how close they live together
2 large populations, people living close together, many international travelers, wealthier countries
3 high-risk countries are in dark blue; low-risk countries are in light blue.

Exercise 4 page 63

Possible causes of pandemics: poor general health, lack of vaccines
Possible factors making a country at high risk: large populations living close together, many international travelers

Exercise 6 page 64

Suggested answers:

1 A vaccine that worked well last year may not be effective this year.
2 A lot of people don't want to have a vaccine that might not work.
3 People spread diseases before they know they have them.
4 It would be impossible to set up a system for checking if people have a disease.
5 It would have a terrible effect on the economy.
6 It would stop a lot of people going to work, and it could separate families.

Exercise 7 page 65

1 b
2 a
3 a

Exercise 8 page 65

3 U
4 A
5 U
6 A
7 A
8 A

Exercise 9 page 65

Answers will vary.

LANGUAGE DEVELOPMENT

Exercise 1 page 66

1 a
2 a
3 a
4 a
5 b
6 b
7 b
8 a

Exercise 2 page 67

1 had developed
2 might not have happened
3 might have survived
4 had found
5 hadn't focused
6 could have discovered
7 had questioned
8 would have realized
9 had allowed
10 wouldn't have called

Exercise 3 page 68

Answers will vary. Possible answers:

2 If I had gotten the flu vaccine
3 If there weren't an outbreak
4 we might need the vaccine
5 he would be prepared

LISTENING 2

Exercise 1 page 69

1 prove
2 clinical
3 researchers
4 precautions
5 scientific
6 controlled
7 data
8 trials

Exercises 2–3 pages 69–70

1 don't agree
2 believe
3 haven't
4 Some

Exercise 4 page 70

Possible answers:

Dr. Sandra Smith: Overall, flu vaccination is a good idea. All medicines should be scientifically proven to be effective. Certain people should definitely take the flu vaccine, such as children, people over 65, pregnant women, and anyone who already has a serious illness.
Mr. Mark Li: The flu vaccine isn't scientifically tested. The flu vaccine can make you sick.

Exercise 6 page 70

1 F; Hundreds of thousands of people get sick from the flu every year.
2 F; The majority of the population does not get vaccinated.
3 T
4 F; He is not against all vaccines, just some.
5 F; There is no scientific evidence that the vaccine doesn't work.
6 F; There is no scientific evidence that the flu vaccine makes people sick.

Exercise 7 page 71

1 d
2 c
3 a
4 e
5 b

Exercise 8 page 71

Answers will vary.

CRITICAL THINKING

Exercises 1–2 pages 72–73

Answers will vary.

Exercise 3 page 73

1 M
2 S
3 S
4 M
5 M
6 S

Exercise 5 page 73

Possible answers:

1 ML: It's natural; it's better than modern medicine; SS: It isn't proven to work; it doesn't help you.
2 ML: This is what people have always done, and it works; SS: Medicine is much more effective than food.
3 ML: They're just trying to make you think you're sick and sell you a cure; SS: It's a valuable way for people to learn about how to treat illnesses.
4 Both: Exercise has been proven to have positive health benefits.
5 ML: The fever is a natural part of the illness; you don't need to give the child medicine; SS: Aspirin will help the child feel better.
6 ML: This may be a good idea, but clinical treatment may still not work for everyone; SS: This is the best thing we can do to prevent illness and disease.

Exercises 6–7 pages 73–74

Answers will vary.

PREPARATION FOR SPEAKING

Exercise 1 page 75

1 d
2 a
3 e
4 b
5 c

Exercises 2–3 page 76

Answers will vary.

ON CAMPUS

Exercise 1 page 78

Answers will vary.

Exercises 2–3 page 78

	cited information (quote, statistic, etc.)	person or organization	title of book or report	date of book or report
1	Poor Americans in some U.S. cities have lower life expectancy than in China or India.	✓	✓	✓
2	More than 600,000 Americans die of heart disease every year.	✓		
3	The death rate from cancer has dropped by 23% since 1991.	✓		✓

Exercise 4 page 79

1 In his book; points out
2 According to
3 A recent report; found

Exercise 5 page 79
Possible answers:
1 In his book *How Doctors Think*, published in 2007, Jerome Groopman points out that on average, doctors interrupt patients 18 seconds after they start to speak.
OR
A recent report, quoted by Jerome Groopman in his book *How Doctors Think*, found that doctors interrupt patients 18 seconds after they start to speak.
2 According to the Centers for Disease Control, most flu-related deaths happen in people over 65.
3 The Austrian philosopher Ivan Illich believed that modern medicine is an institution that serves itself and makes people sick instead of healing them.

UNIT 4
ACTIVATE YOUR KNOWLEDGE
page 81
Answers will vary.

WATCH AND LISTEN
Exercise 1 page 82
Answers will vary.

Exercise 2 page 82
Possible answers:
1 a type of wild cow / a banteng
2 operating on an animal / trying to find a cure for the animal
3 a woolly mammoth; it's extinct

Exercise 3 page 83
b

Exercise 4 page 83
Possible answers:
1 They were able to clone an endangered species.
2 They used the frozen skin cells from a banteng 23 years earlier.
3 It won't help if the animal's natural habitat isn't protected.

Exercise 5 page 83
Answers will vary.

Exercise 6 page 83
Answers will vary.

LISTENING 1
Exercise 1 page 84
1 conservation
2 habitat
3 waste
4 coastal
5 adapt
6 exploit
7 impact
8 modify

Exercise 2 page 85
Group A: main ideas
Group B: details

Exercise 3 page 85
1 c
2 d
3 b
4 a
5 f
6 e

Exercise 5 page 86
Suggested answers:
1 10%
2 natural causes
3 300 square miles
4 rivers were blocked
5 6 million
6 3 ½ million
7 fragmentation
8 fish and other sea life
9 Africa and Asia
10 North America
11 Mumbai
12 diets
13 fruit, plants, nuts, rodents
14 garbage
15 pollution
16 resources
17 waste

Exercise 6 page 87
1 10,000
2 rainforest
3 3 ½
4 1,722,225
5 eating garbage
6 pollution

Exercise 7 page 87
1 a
2 b
3 a

Exercise 8 page 88
3 Humans have changed the <u>Earth</u> …
4 <u>Humans</u> have changed the Earth …
5 Humans <u>have</u> changed the Earth …
6 Humans have <u>changed</u> the Earth …

Exercise 9 page 88
b 2
c 3
d 5
e 1
f 6

Exercise 11 page 88
Answers will vary.

LANGUAGE DEVELOPMENT

Exercise 1 page 89
1 b
2 e
3 a
4 d
5 c

Exercise 2 page 89
1 Based on
2 due to
3 According to
4 instead of
5 as well as
6 except for

Exercise 3 page 89
Answers will vary.

Exercise 4 page 90
1 wrote
2 had spent
3 did
4 had; published
5 began
6 used
7 sprayed
8 had heard
9 decided
10 had released
11 attacked
12 responded

Exercise 5 page 91
1 settled; had been
2 began; had used
3 had not / hadn't noticed; saw
4 erupted; had evacuated
5 created; had been

Exercise 6 page 91
1 adapted
2 survived
3 declined
4 extracted
5 impact
6 affect
7 occurred
8 exploited

LISTENING 2

Exercise 1 page 92
Answers will vary.

Exercise 2 page 92
a mining
b natural gas
c minerals
d diamonds
e harsh
f wilderness
g copper

Exercise 3 page 93
Suggested answers:
1 destruction of deserts
2 exploit
3 ecosystem
4 Soil
5 die
6 dirt and dust
7 manage
8 technological

Exercise 4 page 93
a 6
b 7
c 1
d 8
e 2
f 3
g 5
h 4

Exercise 5 page 93
1 25%
2 North Africa
3 copper, gold, and diamonds
4 hot and dry
5 Arabian oryx
6 solar

Exercise 6 page 94
1 b
2 a
3 c

Exercise 7 page 94
a giving background information
b offering a solution
c explaining a problem

Exercise 8 page 92
Answers will vary.

CRITICAL THINKING

Exercise 1 page 95
Topic: Decline and destruction of deserts
Introduction: <u>Desert environment and wildlife</u>
I. Main idea: <u>Human survival</u>
  A. Detail: <u>People in deserts</u>
    a. Example: Topnaar
    b. Example: Bedouins
  B. Detail: <u>People in cities</u>
II. Main idea: <u>Plant and animal survival</u>
  A. Detail: <u>Desert plants</u>
    a. Example: Acacia tree
  B. Detail: <u>Desert animals</u>
    a. Example: Arabian oryx
Solutions: Manage desert resources carefully instead of abusing them; apply technological solutions; <u>use wind and solar energy</u> to provide clean energy in existing desert cities

Exercise 2 page 96
1 T
2 T
3 F
4 F

Exercises 3–4 page 96
Answers will vary.

PREPARATION FOR SPEAKING

Exercise 1 page 97
1 a
2 b
3 e
4 d
5 f
6 c

Exercise 2 page 98
1 e
2 g
3 d
4 f
5 c
6 a
7 h
8 b

Exercise 3 page 98
1 finishing a section
2 giving examples
3 starting a new section
4 summarizing and concluding
5 introducing the topic
6 querying and analyzing
7 paraphrasing and clarifying
8 giving an overview

ON CAMPUS

Exercise 1 page 100
Answers will vary.

Exercise 2 page 100
1 87%
2 They don't like school work, or they feel overwhelmed.
3 They watch movies or TV, or use social media.
4 Some strategies are: use planners and to-do lists; divide up the work to accomplish a little at a time; plan work at the time of day when they will be most productive.

Exercise 3 page 100
1 g
2 e
3 f
4 d
5 a
6 b
7 c

Exercises 4–8 page 101
Answers will vary.

UNIT 5
ACTIVATE YOUR KNOWLEDGE
page 103
1 This is the Royal Ontario Museum in Toronto, Ontario, Canada.
2–3 *Answers will vary.*

WATCH AND LISTEN

Exercise 1 page 104
Answers will vary.

Exercise 2 page 104
Answers will vary.

Exercise 3 page 105
1 F; Skyscrapers originated in Chicago.
2 T
3 F; The first skyscraper was completed in 1889.
4 F; The skyscraper is considered a symbol of American strength in the world economy.
5 T

Exercise 4 page 105
1 a terrible fire
2 Chicago
3 Michigan Avenue
4 the United States economy
5 corporate success

Exercises 5–6 page 105
Answers will vary.

LISTENING 1

Exercise 1 page 106
a transform
b collapse
c contemporary
d feature
e anticipate
f potential
g obtain
h investment

Exercise 2 page 106
Answers will vary.

Exercise 3 page 107
1 the Westside area itself
2 the poor condition of the warehouse

Exercise 4 page 107
Suggested answers:
1 development; transform
3 Work; potential
4 the area; new modern
5 old architectural
6 contemporary; steel; glass
7 wood, brick; building; building
8 stores, apartments; offices

Exercise 5 page 107
Suggested answers:
1 At the beginning of the conversation, only one developer thinks a building development in Westside is a good idea.
2 There is some development going on in Westside.
3 There has not been much investment in the area in the past 20 years.
4 Only one developer thinks the best idea is to tear down the warehouse.
5 The developers do not need to choose between a contemporary building style and a traditional one.
6 The building can offer floor space for some stores.
7 Stores would not have to be on the second floor.
8 Refurbishment would not mean removing all the original features of the building.

Exercise 6 page 108
1 b   2 d   3 c   4 a

Exercise 7 page 108
Supports knocking the building down:
1, 3; because they have negative connotations
Supports converting and modernizing it:
2, 4; because they have positive connotations

Exercise 8 page 108
Answers will vary.

Exercise 9 page 109
1 It looks like it's <u>probably</u> going to <u>collapse</u>!
2 Really? <u>I</u> think the project is going to be a <u>great success</u>.
3 Couldn't we do <u>both</u>? We'll maintain <u>more</u> of a connection to the <u>past</u> if we include the <u>old building</u> as part of the <u>new one</u>.

Exercise 11 page 109
Answers will vary.

LANGUAGE DEVELOPMENT

Exercise 1 page 110
1 The building I want to move into was bought by a developer. It's <u>certainly</u> going to be renovated before I move there.
2 The construction team <u>probably</u> isn't going to begin work until next month.
3 The supporting walls are already up. The developers will <u>likely</u> complete the building soon.
4 The developer is drawing up his plans now. <u>Maybe</u> he will send me the apartment plans on Friday.
5 I will <u>definitely</u> help you with your architecture homework now.
6 Joe is off from work on Friday. <u>Perhaps</u> he will help you study for the architecture test.

Exercise 2 page 111
Answers will vary.

Exercise 3 page 111
1 contribute
2 transform
3 maintain
4 expand
5 anticipate
6 abandon
7 convert
8 acquire

Exercise 4 page 112

1 expand
2 transform
3 contribute
4 anticipate
5 convert
6 acquire
7 abandon
8 maintain

LISTENING 2

Exercise 1 page 112

a existing
b controversial
c adequate
d sympathetic
e ambitious
f appropriate
g concerned

Exercise 2 page 113
Answers will vary.

Exercise 3 page 113
Answers will vary.

Exercise 4 page 113
Possible answers:
1 Use reflective glass.
2 Reflect the size and materials of the other buildings in the area.
3 Position the new building near the edge of the site.

Exercise 5 page 114

1 C
2 D
3 A
4 B

Exercise 6 page 114

1 D
2 D
3 C
4 C
5 C
6 C
7 D
8 D

Exercise 7 page 115

1 T
2 S
3 T
4 S
5 T
6 S

Exercise 8 page 115
Answers will vary.

CRITICAL THINKING

Exercises 1–2 page 116
Possible answers:

problems	project requirements	solution A	solution B	solution C
crowded apartments	must have more space	✗	✓	✓
200 workers and 50 families need homes	must accommodate all people	✗	✗	✓
too far from school and offices	must be closer	✓	✗	✓
workers must move in one year	must be complete in one year	✓	✓	✓
only $3.8 million to spend	must cost less than $3.8 million	✓	✗	✗

Exercise 3 page 117
Answers will vary.

PREPARATION FOR SPEAKING

Exercise 1 page 118

2 The main <u>issue</u> is that most retailers don't want to do business here.
3 The main issue is that most <u>retailers</u> don't want to do business here.
4 The main issue is that most retailers don't want to do business <u>here</u>.

Exercise 2 page 118

a 3
b 1
c 4
d 2

Exercise 3 pages 118–119

1 We need to find a way around the problem of high prices.
2 The problem is that we don't have enough time.
3 The main issue is that people don't like our design.
4 We need to find a way around the problem of attracting business.
5 The main issue is that the building is collapsing.
6 The problem is that no one wants to live in the area.

Exercise 4 page 119
Answers will vary. Possible answers:
1 Could we increase the budget?
2 Can I suggest we increase the budget?
3 Should we consider increasing the budget?
4 How about increasing the budget?
5 Have you thought about increasing the budget?
6 Why don't we increase the budget?

Exercise 5 page 119
Answers will vary. Possible answers:
1 Could we build a parking lot?
2 Can I suggest we reduce the height?
3 Should we consider turning the wasteland into a park?
4 How about building a rooftop garden?
5 Have you thought about having more, larger units?
6 Why don't we offer lower rents?

Exercise 6 page 120
1 reject
2 accept
3 accept
4 reject
5 reject
6 accept

Exercise 7 page 120
Answers will vary.

ON CAMPUS

Exercise 2 page 122
1 making time to study
2 choosing classes
3 participating in class
4 relationships with teachers

Exercise 3 page 122

advice	reasons
1 Keep up with course work	There are many quizzes and tests Students are supposed to work on their own
2 Take a class in a new subject	Explore your interests Get to know different fields of study
3 Ask questions in class	Helps the class Professors expect it You get a better grade
4 Get to know your professors	Shows that you're interested You can learn a lot from them Sometimes you can help with research

Exercises 4–5 page 123
Answers will vary.

Exercise 6 page 123
1 b
2 e
3 a
4 d
5 c

Exercise 7 page 123
Answers will vary.

UNIT 6
ACTIVATE YOUR KNOWLEDGE
page 125
Answers will vary.

WATCH AND LISTEN

Exercise 1 page 126
Answers will vary.

Exercise 2 page 126
Answers will vary.

Exercise 3 page 127
1 T
2 F; Their electric bills have been greatly reduced.
3 F; Solar panels can reduce a home's energy consumption by 70%.
4 T
5 F; They don't spend any time watching their meter.

Exercise 4 page 127
1 Their bill is 70% less.
2 He has built over 150 homes.
3 Panels will soon be more efficient so that they will be usable in states with short days and less light.

Exercise 5 page 127
Answers will vary.

Exercise 6 page 127
Answers will vary.

LISTENING 1

Exercise 1 page 128
1 element
2 consistent
3 reservoir
4 mainland
5 cycle
6 network
7 generate
8 capacity

Exercise 2 page 129
1 Government
2 Population
3 Area
4 Mainland

Exercise 3 page 129
Answers will vary.

Exercise 4 page 129
1 c
2 a
3 c

Exercise 5 page 130
1 seafood restaurant
2 five years
3 Madrid
4 tough
5 relaxing
6 the sea
7 quiet
8 traffic
9 banking
10 independent
11 oil
12 40,000
13 mainland
14 over 2 million dollars

Exercise 6 pages 130–131
1 3,000
2 30
3 wind turbines
4 11
5 3,500
6 water
7 dam
8 volcano
9 17 million
10 2,297
11 sea level
12 cycle
13 hill
14 drinking
15 agriculture
16 seawater
17 mainland

Exercise 7 page 131
1 MT
2 D
3 D
4 D
5 D
6 MT

Exercise 8 page 131
1 b
2 c
3 a

Exercise 9 page 132
a 2
b 3
c 1

Exercise 11 page 132
1 sadness
2 excitement
3 excitement
4 surprise
5 annoyance

Exercise 13 page 132
Answers will vary.

LANGUAGE DEVELOPMENT

Exercise 1 page 133
giving extra information
In addition,
Moreover,
Furthermore,
comparing and contrasting
Even so,
Nevertheless,
explaining a result
therefore
and as a result

Exercise 2 page 134
Answers will vary. Possible answers:
1 City life is stressful. On the other hand, island life is relaxing.
2 The houses use solar electricity. Furthermore, they have water-recycling systems.
3 Dams can damage habitats. As a result, they have to be planned carefully.
4 The wind blows for 30% of the year. Nevertheless, that isn't enough to provide all of the island's electricity.
5 This electric car can go just over 62 miles per hour. Moreover, the battery can be charged using solar power.
6 The system requires that water moves from a high place to a lower place, so we've placed a water tank on a hill.

Exercise 3 page 135
1 P
2 P
3 A
4 P
5 A
6 A

Exercise 4 page 135

1 is used
2 is created
3 is found
4 be extracted
5 are caused
6 are drilled
7 is supplied
8 can be used

Exercise 5 page 135

1 generation
2 element
3 capacity
4 source
5 challenge
6 network
7 potential
8 decline

LISTENING 2

Exercise 1 page 136

Answers will vary. Possible answers:
1 computers, lights, photocopiers, printers, coffee machines, etc.
2 turn off screens on computers when not using them, turn off lights when no one is in a room, etc.

Exercise 2 page 136

1 consumption
2 maintenance
3 experimental
4 efficient
5 limitation
6 function
7 volume
8 drawback

Exercise 3 page 137

speaker	proposed solutions	large-scale
Zara	Install [1] solar panels on the roof	✓
Allen	Change to [2] low-energy lightbulbs	
Abdul	Clean dirty windows to get more [3] natural light	
	Turn off [4] computer screens when get up from desk	
Zara	Turn off [5] air-conditioning when it isn't hot	
	Get rid of one [6] photocopier	
	Install a solar [7] water heating system	✓

Exercise 4 page 137

1 solar panels
2 quickly
3 Cleaning
4 two
5 air conditioning
6 maintenance
7 green
8 simple

Exercise 5 page 138

1 b
2 d
3 a
4 e
5 c

Exercise 6 page 139

1 d
2 c
3 e
4 b
5 a

Exercise 7 page 139

Answers will vary.

CRITICAL THINKING

Exercise 1 page 140

solar panels, low-energy lightbulbs, clean dirty windows, turn off computer screens, turn off air conditioning, get rid of one photocopier, solar water heating system; large-scale solutions: solar panels and solar water-heating system

Exercise 2 page 140

Answers will vary.

Exercises 3–4 page 140

Answers will vary.

PREPARATION FOR SPEAKING

Exercise 1 page 141
1 b
2 a
3 c

Exercises 2–3 page 141
1 c
2 a
3 b

Exercise 4 page 142
Answers will vary. Possible answers:
1 Could you please wait until I've finished speaking?
2 Would you mind explaining what you mean?
3 That isn't really what we're talking about.
4 Sorry, but would you mind waiting until Tom finishes speaking?

Exercise 5 page 142
3 A
4 N
5 N
6 A

ON CAMPUS

Exercise 1 page 144
Answers will vary.

Exercise 2 page 144
c

Exercise 3 page 144
Suggested answers:
1 the ability to work well with other people
2 collaborating, listening to other people's opinions, asking questions, respecting differences and resolving conflicts
3 the project is not clearly defined enough; people feel that their opinions are not valued; people complain that a majority of the work is done by a minority of the people
4 make sure the project has a clear timeline; divide up the work and give everyone a specific job to do
5 according to what people are good at
6 a designer, a leader, and a recorder

Exercise 5 page 145
1 technical expert
2 communicator
3 recorder
4 reporter
5 group leader
6 chairperson

Exercise 6 page 145
1 *Suggested answers:*
A language expert helps with translation or writing.
A timekeeper makes sure that meetings start and end on time; keeps members aware of important deadlines.
A harmonizer makes sure that every member of the group feels valued; works to keep the group working well.
An information gatherer does research for the project or finds out about local resources.
2–4 *Answers will vary.*

UNIT 7
ACTIVATE YOUR KNOWLEDGE
page 147
Answers will vary.

WATCH AND LISTEN

Exercise 1 page 148
Answers will vary.

Exercise 2 page 148
Answers will vary.

Exercise 3 page 149
1 b
2 c
3 a

Exercise 4 page 149
1 perspective
2 encourage
3 light up
4 networked

Exercise 5 page 149
1 uses new technologies
2 allows viewer to reflect and interact
3 allows the viewer to only reflect
4 uses paint and other similar materials

Exercise 6 page 149
Answers will vary.

LISTENING 1

Exercise 1 page 150
a identity
b right
c remove
d self-expression
e comment
f composition
g creativity
h criticism

Exercise 2 page 151
Answers will vary.

Exercise 3 page 151
1 c
2 a
3 a yes
  b no
  c yes
  d yes
  e yes

Exercise 4 page 151
Answers will vary. Possible answers:
Alex: interesting to look at, distinctive style, decorates the area
office worker: no right to spray paint their message, art is in a museum
police officer: creative, expressive, should get permission
Simone: expressive, color and composition work well, could make a lot of money
Joseph: wishes he'd done it, good way of expressing ideas, communicates a message

Exercise 5 page 152
a 3
b 2
c 1
d 2
e 4
f 1
g 5
h 5
i 4
j 3

Exercise 6 page 152
1 very creative, the artist, a piece of art, artistic, expressive, artwork
2 vandalism, the area's mystery graffiti artist, our illegal painter, this piece of vandalism
3 *Answers will vary. Possible answer:* The police officer seems to like the painting more. The police officer's personal and professional opinions are different. The host should be neutral but seems to dislike the graffiti.

Exercise 7 page 153
3 com-<u>mu</u>-ni-cate – com-mu-ni-<u>ca</u>-tion
4 cre-<u>ate</u> – cre-<u>a</u>-tion
5 ex-<u>hib</u>-it – ex-hi-<u>bi</u>-tion
6 re-com-<u>mend</u> – re-com-men-<u>da</u>-tion
7 ac-<u>tiv</u>-i-ty – <u>ac</u>-tive
8 <u>ar</u>-tist – ar-<u>tis</u>-tic

Exercise 9 page 153
Answers will vary.

LANGUAGE DEVELOPMENT

Exercise 1 page 154
1 who; <u>Ray Noland</u>
2 whose; <u>The people</u>
3 where; <u>The museum</u>
4 when; <u>Mondays</u>

Exercise 2 pages 154–155
2 NI – The painting includes Marianne, <u>who represents the victory of the French Republic over the monarchy.</u>
3 NI – Marianne, <u>whose image also appears on small stamps and euro coins</u>, is also depicted as a statue at Place de la République in Paris.
4 NI – Botticelli's *Venus with Three Graces*, <u>which is also located in the Louvre</u>, is a fresco.
5 I – Fresco is a method of painting <u>that is done with water-based paints on wet plaster</u>.
6 I – The painting <u>that Botticelli painted on the walls of the Tuscan Villa Lemmi</u> is located in the same room as Luini's *Adoration of the Magi*.
7 I – People <u>who visit the Louvre</u> can use cameras and video recorders, but not flash photography.
8 I – The Louvre is the museum <u>where parts of the movie</u> *The Da Vinci Code* were filmed.

LISTENING 2

Exercise 1 page 155
1 appreciate
2 analyze
3 focus
4 display
5 interpret
6 reject
7 restore
8 reveal

Exercise 2 page 156
Answers will vary.

Exercise 3 page 156
Answers will vary. Possible answers:
Robert: they need to find out how much new art would cost, thinks Pei is right, they need to do more research
Lisa: not really sure that paying for art is an appropriate way to spend public money, the art doesn't really benefit the city's population more people would use and benefit from a recreation center, public art is a waste of money
Ahmad: art is an important part of any culture, Art can help make us proud of our city, the location of the artwork rather than the artwork itself is the problem, moving it might solve the vandalism problem, children need to see art in public places, balance investment in leisure activities and public art
Marco: art can have a very positive effect on people

Pei: not sure a rec center would be popular enough, consider moving the sculpture, could be a tourist attraction

Claudia: public safety issue, artwork really is causing more problems than it's worth

Exercise 4 page 156
Check: 1, 3, 5, 6, 8

Exercise 5 page 157
Suggested answers:
1 what new art will cost
2 analyze the pieces we like
3 gather data and opinions
4 a survey
5 climb on the public art
6 the location
7 a different location
8 choose a new project
9 see public art
10 explore options

Exercise 6 page 158
1 F
2 O
3 F
4 F
5 O
6 O
7 F
8 O

Exercise 7 page 158
Answers will vary.

Exercise 8 page 158
Answers will vary.

CRITICAL THINKING

Exercise 1 page 159
1 a
2 b
3 d
4 c

Exercise 2 page 160
Answers will vary.

Exercise 3 page 160
Answers will vary.

Exercises 4–5 page 160
Answers will vary.

PREPARATION FOR SPEAKING

Exercise 1 page 161
1 The speaker thinks it's a piece of art.
2 This looks like
3 but in fact

Exercise 3 page 162
2 Many people think that public art has no long-term cost. However, cleaning and maintenance need to be considered.
3 It seems like the new sculpture is very popular, but actually a thousand people have signed a petition to have it removed.
4 It looks like the government wasted a lot of money on the sculpture. The fact of the matter is it was donated to the city.

Exercise 4 page 162
1 C
2 A
3 A
4 C

Exercise 5 page 163
Answers will vary.

Exercise 6 page 163
Answers will vary.

Exercise 7 page 164
Answers will vary.
2 <u>I'm</u> not an expert, but …
3 All <u>I</u> know is …
4 For <u>me</u>, …
5 You <u>could</u> say that; however <u>actually</u> …
6 That's true <u>in part</u>, but <u>I</u> think …
7 You <u>may</u> be right, but <u>I</u> wonder if …
8 <u>I see</u> what you're saying, but <u>maybe</u> …

Exercise 8 page 164
Answers will vary.

ON CAMPUS

Exercise 1 page 166
Answers will vary.

Exercise 2 page 166
your interests

Exercise 3 pages 166–167
1 T
2 DNS
3 F; It's good to think about how you might make a living, but students have to be realistic about their skills and abilities.
4 T
5 DNS
6 T
7 F; Many people don't find work in their major field, and most people change their careers several times.
8 T

Exercise 4 page 167
Answers will vary.

Exercise 5 page 167

1 c, e
2 a, d
3 b, f

UNIT 8
ACTIVATE YOUR KNOWLEDGE
page 169
Answers will vary.

WATCH AND LISTEN

Exercise 1 page 170
Answers will vary.

Exercise 2 page 170
Answers will vary.

Exercise 3 page 171
1 F; Gordon and Peggy live in a retirement community 45 miles from Phoenix.
2 T
3 F; 86% of boomers believe that are more active than their parents were in retirement.
4 T

Exercise 4 page 171
1 b
2 d
3 c
4 a

Exercise 5 page 171
1 a
2 b
3 a

Exercise 6 page 171
Answers will vary.

LISTENING 1

Exercise 1 page 172
Answers will vary.

Exercise 2 page 172
1 retirement
2 generations
3 permit
4 dependents
5 ensure
6 pension
7 property
8 assets

Exercise 3 page 173
Check: 1, 3, 6, 7

Exercise 4 page 173
1 25 trillion
2 36
3 26
4 65
5 272,000
6 2/3
7 16

Exercise 5 page 174
3 S
4 S
5 G
6 S
7 G
8 G

Exercise 6 page 175

	vowels joined with /y/	vowels joined with /w/	dropped /d/	dropped /t/
1			✓	
2		✓		
3			✓	
4		✓		
5	✓			
6				✓
7			✓	

Exercise 8 page 175
Answers will vary.

LANGUAGE DEVELOPMENT

Exercise 1 pages 176–177
1 We always advise our daughters *to* enjoy life.
2 We want *to* encourage to other people to retire early.
3 We managed *to* save enough money when we were working.
4 We would *not to consent to going* into a retirement home.
5 We refuse *to* spend our retirement at home.
6 I won't force to my children *to* take care of me.
7 We do not need to avoid *retiring* because we saved a lot of money when we were working.
8 The financial adviser wants that you *to work* until you are 65 years old.

Exercise 2 page 177

1 to visit
2 going
3 to meet
4 to babysit
5 working
6 gardening
7 to save
8 playing

Exercise 3 page 177

Answers will vary. Possible answers:
2 My wife didn't agree to accept the idea at first.
3 Her generous pension allows her to retire comfortably.
4 We would never threaten to leave our children without any inheritance.

LISTENING 2

Exercise 1 page 178

1 b
2 a
3 b
4 c
5 c
6 b
7 a
8 c

Exercises 2–3 page 179

Answers will vary.

Exercise 4 page 179

Answers will vary. Possible answers:

Mika, Japan	Ahmet, Turkey
Importance of family: – extended family Figures explaining how population is changing: – Highest life expectancy in the world – Low fertility rate – People wait longer to get married – Fewer young people to care for elderly – More care centers Solution: – Government has citizens pay income tax to help elderly	Most elderly living in household Drawbacks: – Caregivers and old people aren't free to do what they like – Older people don't like how things are done – Living closely together causes tensions Benefits: – Older people help with domestic jobs and childcare – Older people have a sense of responsibility Challenge: – Elderly population is growing Solution: – Continue caring for elderly at home

Exercise 5 page 179

1 Mika: Japan; Ahmet: Turkey
2 Mika
3 Ahmet
4 **Mika:** Importance of family in her country, how population is changing with fewer young people, and how government is helping by making citizens pay a tax

Ahmet: Drawbacks and benefits of older people living in households with younger people, challenges of the situation, and possible solutions

Exercise 6 page 180

	Mika	Ahmet
country	Japan	Turkey
population today	127 million	80 million
% 65 or older today	26%	6%
% of households with older people	*no information*	80%
expected population in 2050	107 million	*no information*
expected % 60 or older in 2050	42.5%	*no information*

Exercise 7 page 180

1 E
2 C
3 E
4 C
5 E
6 E

Exercise 8 page 180

Answers will vary.

CRITICAL THINKING

Exercise 1 page 181

1 approximately 29 million
2 approximately 17 million
3 approximately 24 million
4 ages 15 to 54
5 people 14 and under

Exercise 2 page 182

Answers will vary. Possible answers:
The 0–14 population will continue to decline.
The 15–64 population will also decline more.
The over-65 population will decrease, but more slowly.

Exercise 3 page 182

1 *Answers will vary. Possible answers:*

Country A:
Increasing total population
Increasing over-65 population

Country B:
Decreasing total population
Rising and then falling over-65 population

Country C:
Increasing total population
Fairly steady over-65 population

2 *Answers will vary.*

Exercise 4 page 183

Answers will vary.

Exercise 5 page 183

Answers will vary.

PREPARATION FOR SPEAKING

Exercise 1 page 184

1 B
2 A
3 A
4 B
5 A
6 B

Exercise 2 page 185

Answers will vary.

Exercise 3 page 185

1 c *or* e
2 c *or* e
3 a
4 b
5 d

Exercise 4 page 186

Answers will vary. Possible answers:

1 People living longer can be traced back to improvements in medical care.
2 A population decrease was the result of people moving out of the country.
3 A population increase was brought about by an increase in people over 65.
4 The steady population was the result of the high number of people over 65.

Exercise 5 page 186

2 The population of country B will be <u>77 million</u> in 2050. This number is <u>much larger than</u> the population figure of <u>1.4 million</u> for country A in 2050.
3 By 2050, country A's population will rise to <u>1.78 million</u> people. The population for country B <u>also</u> peaks in 2050 with <u>9.2 million</u> people.

ON CAMPUS

Exercise 1 page 188

1 graduate school
2 job fair
3 network
4 résumé
5 internship

Exercise 2 page 188

The speaker mentions the following services:
Job Listings
Workshops: résumé writing, your online identity
Upcoming job fairs
Graduate Schools

Exercise 3 page 189

1 Part-time jobs on and off campus.
2 It's good experience, and can lead to a paid position.
3 Work experience, and community service or leadership positions.
4 Employers look at profiles on social media before calling candidates for an interview.
5 Network, ask questions, and find out about future opportunities.
6 Students can research different graduate programs and find out about financial aid.

Exercise 4 page 189

Answers will vary.

Exercise 5 page 189

Suggested answers:

1 Job listings; workshop "Strategies for a successful interview"
2 Work and study abroad; volunteer opportunities
3 Graduate schools; internships or job fairs
4 "Lecture: Working in the software industry"; job fairs
5 Workshop "Résumé Writing for College Students"; job fairs

Exercise 6 page 189

Answers will vary.

UNIT 1

▶ **NBA Fans in China**

Seth Doane (reporter):   Good morning to you, Norah. That's right. By the end of this season, the NBA will have put together almost 150 of these international games since 1978. They're a way of building the brand overseas. To call this crowd enthusiastic would be an understatement. Security struggled to keep back fans as the Lakers entered. It felt more like Southern California than Shanghai in this stadium, where the language of sport proved universal.

Fan: Kobe ... Kobe Bryant! I love Kobe so much!

Seth Doane: An injured Kobe Bryant did not play much at Thursday's fan appreciation night, though that did not seem to matter. Kobe is huge here. The NBA says viewership in China grew 30% last year. NBA Commissioner David Stern pointed out that these 13,000 people came to watch a practice.

David Stern: China is our largest market outside the United States. It has 1.3 billion people and has been playing basketball for almost as long as the United States has.

Seth Doane: Players took in some of the sights and toured the Great Wall earlier this week. It was Golden State Warriors' point guard Stephen Curry's first trip to China.

Stephen Curry: I knew that they loved the game of basketball but to see them, you know, with Warrior jerseys everywhere, it's awesome.

Seth Doane: "Awesome" could have described the night for Xiao Wei, who unfurled a banner for Curry. Rough translation, "god of cuteness."

How was it to meet him to talk with him in person?

Xiao Wei: It's beyond imagination.

Seth Doane: Making the NBA feel closer and, of course, boosting partnerships and endorsement deals is part of the mission for David Stern.

David Stern: You see opportunity everywhere, although China is going to become the largest economy in the world in the not too distant future, so that's pretty impressive of what we're going to do.

Seth Doane: So it's important for you all to be here.

David Stern: Actually, I'm surprised that Charlie Rose isn't here doing the morning news because he's a, he's a big jock.

Seth Doane: Charlie would love to be here, I think. Yes, that's right. And the NBA expects to see double-digit revenue growth every year here in China, well

into the future. Last year it's estimated they hauled in around 150 million dollars in China alone. You like whose name came, comes up courtside in Shanghai, Charlie and Norah?

Norah O'Donnell: Love that. I just have one request, Seth, and that is that banner, that "god of cuteness." Can you get one of those for me so I can get it for Charlie? He's my god of cuteness.

Seth Doane: All right, I'll look in the market downstairs.

Charlie Rose: Oh, goodness. Boy, this is great. This is really great.

Norah O'Donnell: You would have loved to have been there.

Charlie Rose: I would have. Oh, yeah. I mean I did a profile of Jeremy Lin for CBS Sports, and it's just remarkable the intensity when he went back, and how much they love him, and how all that Rockets games are now seen in China.

Norah O'Donnell: Absolutely.

◀ **1.1**

Host: Today on *The World Close Up* – "The 11,000-Mile Fruit Salad." With globalization, the world has become a smaller place. On last week's show, we talked about how people around the world are watching foreign TV shows, wearing clothes from other countries, and working at companies with several international offices. On this week's show, let's look at how globalization allows us to taste food from different cultures around the world, without leaving the country. We don't just mean specialty products, like Turkish candies and Japanese desserts. Think about the regular groceries customers are buying every day. Where do they come from? How do they get to your supermarket? And what is the true *environmental* cost of your usual grocery list? Our reporter Darren Hayes has gone to a Food King Supermarket in southern Philadelphia to **investigate** this issue and to see just what *countries* customers are putting in their shopping carts.

Reporter: Hello, listeners. I'm here at the Food King Supermarket in southern Philadelphia. There are a lot of healthy **consumers** here, and David Green is one of them. David, can we take a look in your shopping cart? What are you buying today?

David: Mostly fruit and vegetables. I have a pineapple, some bananas, some kiwis, a mango, and tomatoes. I'm making a fruit salad for lunch because I'm watching my weight. I'm trying to eat healthfully.

Reporter: I notice on the label that the bananas are from Ecuador.

David: Yeah ... so?

Reporter: Do you mind if I check the pineapple? Hmmm ... it's from Guatemala. The kiwi comes from ... California, and the mango is from Costa Rica. David, did you realize that some of this fruit is **imported** from **overseas**?

David: Well, I guess since it's winter, we can't grow these everywhere in our country. They *have* to be imported. If they weren't, then how would we get fresh fruit in the winter?

Reporter: Good point. The global food industry – and the speed of shipping fresh foods by air – allows people all over the world to eat a huge variety of fresh fruit and vegetables all year round.

David: It's just more convenient, isn't it? Most of the fruit and vegetables I like, like peppers, mangoes, and bananas, grow in hotter climates. A lot of the fruit and vegetables that grow here in the northern part of the United States only grow in the summer.

Reporter: It *is* possible to grow fruit and vegetables from hot countries here, but they have to grow in **greenhouses** or certain parts of the country, which increases production costs. If you look at these tomatoes, which were grown on a local farm, they're almost twice the cost of the tomatoes you have here from Mexico, over 2,000 miles away.

David: I'd never pay that for a few tomatoes! Local food can be so expensive. It's not worth it.

Reporter: I know, but cheap food comes at a price. Let's look at the figures. The bananas from Ecuador must have traveled more than 2,500 miles to reach Food King Supermarket, the pineapple from Guatemala must have come more than 2,000 miles, and the Costa Rican mango nearly 2,200 miles. The kiwi from California? That must have flown about 2,300 miles. So, that's about ... 11,000 miles of air travel in one bowl! That's an incredibly long food supply chain, which is the system and things involved in the moving of a product from the place it is **produced** to the person who buys it. It's also a huge carbon footprint, which means a huge amount of pollution was produced to get this food to the shelves. When food travels, a lot of carbon dioxide pollution is produced, and most people now believe that carbon dioxide in the air is causing climate change – causing the Earth to get generally warmer.

David: I've never really thought about it that much. What about this lettuce? It's local.

Reporter: Even something that looks like it's local can have a big impact on the environment. It's far cheaper for supermarkets to have several large factories than a lot of small ones all over the country, so food grown around the country is transported to large factories to be packaged and sold. This lettuce may be local, but the farm it came from could have transported it across the country and then put it into this plastic packaging. It's sometimes then transported back to the place it was grown in the first place.

David: So, before arriving at Food King Supermarket, this local lettuce might have traveled ...

Reporter: ... maybe 300 miles? You can only really be sure how far something has traveled if you **purchase** it directly from a farm or if you grow it yourself.

David: Wow. I can't believe it. Maybe I should pay the extra money for local food ...

Reporter: Thanks for your time, David. An 11,000-mile fruit salad that comes from five different countries isn't very expensive for the consumer. But the big question is, what's the true environmental cost of such a well-traveled salad? That's all for today. Thanks for listening to *The World, Close Up*.

🔊 **1.2**

1 ... cheap food comes at a price.
2 An 11,000-mile fruit salad ...
3 ... what's the true environmental cost of such a well-traveled salad?

🔊 **1.3**

1 These agricultural products are already going abroad.
2 We grow many kinds of tea on this plantation.
3 The police regularly find illegal imports.
4 The company sewed more clothes overseas last year.
5 The bananas are timed so that they ripen together.
6 Flying the crops causes air pollution.
7 The products pass through customs easily.
8 I want to know why these routes cost more.

🔊 **1.4**

There hasn't been much support from the government over the issue of imported agricultural crops. There are three issues with this. First, nearly a sixth of all imported fruit cannot grow in our climate. Second, the state should help our own farmers rather than foreign growers. Finally, we should not fall into the trap of not growing enough food. What would happen if it didn't rain and we were left with a food shortage?

🔊 **1.5**

As globalization becomes more of a reality in our everyday lives, we can see it taking root in all aspects of life. Foreign trade and imports range from the TV shows we watch and love to the food we eat and the clothes we wear every day.

As a result, it's easier than ever to find a wide variety of imported goods in our local shops and markets. But is global trade actually unhealthy for the environment?

There has been a lot of discussion in the media about imported products, and especially imported foods. Many people say that imported products may in fact harm the environment because they're shipped long distances by airplane. It has been suggested that we should choose **domestic** foods over overseas **exports** because airplanes create pollution that causes environmental problems.

Let's look at food, for instance. Experts argue that foods that are the least damaging to the environment are usually the ones grown locally. Consequently, some people believe that local foods are always more environmentally friendly and, therefore, must always be the most appropriate choice, but is this really true? Let's look at some data.

This pie chart shows the carbon footprint of the U.S. food system. First, as you can see, the largest part of the carbon footprint is the section called "**Households**," meaning the energy used in homes to store and prepare food – mostly refrigeration and cooking with gas or electrical appliances. This accounts for more than a quarter of the total carbon footprint. Second, according to the chart, the next main **source** of carbon in the U.S. food system is how companies **process** their products. Examples of this would be adding chemicals to vegetables so that they can be put into cans, or turning ingredients into ready-made meals, like frozen pizza. This makes up about one-fifth of the total. After processing, **agriculture** is the next main source of carbon emissions. Parts of the United States are cool and rainy, which means that some avocados in the U.S. must grow in greenhouses. These greenhouses are heated, which therefore produces carbon dioxide. Avocados grown in Mexico require less energy to grow because the climate in Mexico is milder, and greenhouses aren't needed.

After agriculture, wholesale and retail food sales account for 14% of the food carbon footprint. This refers to the energy used to store and sell foods in warehouses and supermarkets and so on.

After that comes food service. This basically means the energy used by restaurants and cafés to supply food to customers. Next comes emissions linked to packaging such as the containers that food is put in to be sold or transported. For example, when you purchase chicken in a U.S. supermarket, it comes in a tray and is usually wrapped in plastic. Finally, the smallest portion of energy in the U.S. food system goes to **transportation**. So, what does this tell us about food miles? In summary, the data shows that the transportation of food definitely uses energy and produces carbon emissions, but from this evidence, we can assume that it must make up the very smallest part of the carbon footprint from food.

 1.6

I'd like to talk about where your money goes when you buy a cup of coffee. There has been a lot of discussion in the media recently about fair prices for the people in countries that grow crops like coffee. Many people believe that it's not right that a cup of coffee can cost $4 or more, of which the farmers only get a few pennies. However, others have pointed out that the coffee beans are only one part of the cost of supplying a cup of coffee. They say that the other ingredients, such as milk and sugar, are also a big part of the cost of a cup of coffee. However, I would like to show that in a typical coffeehouse, the ingredients are only a small part of the overall cost. Let's look at some data. If you consider the information in this chart …

1.7

This pie chart shows where your money goes when you buy a cup of coffee. First, as you can see, the largest part of the cost is administration, at approximately 25%. That's a quarter of the cost per cup. Second is labor, which you'll notice accounts for almost 20% of the cost. Next, tax, profit, and rent each make up about 14% of the cost, or a total of 42% of the price of your cup of coffee. Finally, I'd like to draw your attention to the three parts that are related to the product you take away – milk at over 6%, the cup, sugar, and lid at almost 5%, and the coffee itself at 2%. Together, they make up just over 10% of the price you pay.

1.8

Hello everyone. You probably know that hunger is a problem in many parts of the world. But at the same time, tons of food are thrown away every year, in landfills like the one in the picture. Today I'm going to talk a little bit about food waste and what we can do about it.

First, let's see if you can answer this question: what percentage of food is thrown away in the United States every year? What do you think? Raise your hand if you think it's 10% … 20? 30%? … More than 30%? You're right. In fact, 40% of the food that is bought in the U.S. is wasted. This is more than 20 pounds of food per person, per month.

Why is this a problem? Well, for one thing, consumer-driven food waste in the U.S. costs approximately 165 billion dollars a year. But did you know that food waste also contributes to climate change? This is because the organic waste in our landfills emits methane, a gas that contributes to greenhouse gases. So throwing food away is expensive in terms of the waste of resources, and also it's bad for the environment.

But there's another reason: the world simply cannot afford to throw food away. As you know, hunger is a growing problem. Worldwide, more than 900 million people suffer from hunger, and the numbers are rising.

The Food and Agriculture Organization estimates that by the year 2050, we will need about 170 million more acres of farmland to feed our growing population. If we could reduce consumer-driven food waste by just 30% – that's just over a quarter – we could save roughly 100 million acres of farmland.

So, cutting food waste is a very important step towards improving the global supply of food.

What can we do to fight food waste? Well, I'm going to talk about three ways that we can all work to …

🔊 1.9

Excerpt 1

Hello everyone. You probably know that hunger is a problem in many parts of the world. But at the same time, tons of food are thrown away every year, in landfills like the one in the picture.

Excerpt 2

First, let's see if you can answer this question: what percentage of food is thrown away in the United States every year? What do you think? Raise your hand if you think it's 10% … 20? 30%?

Excerpt 3

Why is this a problem? Well, for one thing, consumer-driven food waste in the U.S. costs approximately 165 billion dollars a year. But did you know that food waste also contributes to climate change?

Excerpt 4

As you know, hunger is a growing problem. Worldwide, more than 900 million people suffer from hunger, and the numbers are rising.

Excerpt 5

If we could reduce consumer-driven food waste by just 30% – that's just over a quarter – we could save roughly 100 million acres of farmland.

UNIT 2

▶ A Soybean-Powered Car

Reporter: The star at last week's Philadelphia auto show wasn't a sports car or an economy car. It was a sports economy car. Performance and practicality under a single hood: car buyers had been waiting decades for this.

Man 1: Anything going zero to 60 in four seconds – that piques my interest.

Man 2: Yeah. I didn't think you could do that with a hybrid.

Man 3: I like that it does get 51 miles to a gallon.

Reporter: And on soybean biodiesel to boot.

Man 4: This is fabulous, what they've done.

Man 3: I think they did one hell of a job.

Reporter: So, who do we have to thank? Ford? Toyota? Ferrari? Nope. Just Victor, David, Cheeseborough, Bruce, and Cozy. These high school auto shop students, along with a handful of other kids from West Philadelphia High School, built the car as an after-school project. It took them over a year, rummaging for parts, configuring wires, learning as they went.

Simon Houger: All these rubber mounts can mount the motor to the frame.

Reporter: Impressed? Teacher Simon Houger says, wait until you hear this.

Simon Houger: We have a number of high school dropouts. We have a number that have been removed for disciplinary reasons and they end up with us.

Reporter: Cozy Harmon was in a gang at his old school, a punk, and a terrible student.

Cozy Harmon: Grades. I was just getting by the skin of my teeth, Cs and Ds. I came here and now I'm a straight-A student.

Reporter: Really?

Cozy Harmon: Yes, sir.
Check the brakes. Put the pop up.

Simon Houger: If you give kids that have been stereotyped as not being able to do anything an opportunity to do something great, they'll step up.

Cozy Harmon: Hey, ah, Clayton, brake fluid. Cool.

Reporter: Obviously, this story says a lot about the potential of our young people. Unfortunately, it also says a lot about our auto industry, now stuck playing hybrid catch-up to the bad news bears of auto shop.

Simon Houger: Yeah. It hit me that, look, we made this work. We're not geniuses, so why aren't other people doing it?

Reporter: Cozy thinks he knows. It's big oil companies.

Cozy Harmon: Right. They're making billions upon billions of dollars, right, and then when this car sells, their billions upon billions will go down to low billions upon billions.

🔊 2.1

Ada: Hello, I'm Ada. Are you my **advisor**?

Advisor: Yes, Ada. Welcome to the advising office. Good to see you.

Ada: Hi.

Advisor: Now, I saw from your file that you're looking for advice on what to major in. Do you have any ideas?

Ada: Yes, but I'm not really sure which to choose.

Advisor: Well, what are you considering?

Ada: I like math and physics, and I'm doing well in those classes.

Advisor: Looking at your file, I couldn't agree more! You should make use of your math and physics abilities. Any ideas about what you want to study?

Ada: Well, I'm considering studying engineering.

Advisor: Ah, engineering. That's a big subject area field. Well, engineering jobs are definitely popular. The world will always need engineers! What kind of engineering are you interested in? Electrical? Civil? Computer?

Ada: I'm not sure. I've always been interested in the way things work, like cars and other machines. I'd like to study something technical, that's for sure. You know, I'm actually really interested in space flight. I'd love to build rockets and spacecraft!

Advisor: Maybe you should consider **mechanical** engineering, then – as a start anyway. That's a good, basic engineering degree – it covers the basic subjects. Mechanical engineers often go on to become **specialists** in lots of different areas – aerospace engineering is just one of them. It would definitely be a way to use your math and physics skills. You'd also **acquire** some really useful new skills and an in-depth **understanding** of the field.

Ada: Okay, but I'm not sure if that would be for me. An engineering major would be very **academic**. I wonder if I should try something more **vocational**. I actually like manual work better. I'd rather make something than write about it! Is it possible to do both? Maybe I could do an **internship** at an engineering company and then study after I see how the internship goes.

Advisor: Of course, you should consider an internship, but it would be helpful to take some engineering courses too. Have you done much research on different courses that are available?

Ada: Not yet.

Advisor: I suggest that you try to find out more about engineering courses. I could give you the names of some professors who teach the introductory engineering courses. You could talk to them and maybe even visit one of their classes.

Ada: Yes, that's a good idea. I think I could do that. I'd like to know more about what engineers actually do, and I'd rather talk to someone than just read the information on websites. Thanks.

Advisor: In that case, have you considered talking to some engineers about their work?

Ada: I don't know any engineers.

Advisor: Well, there are several engineering companies that will be at the college career fair next week. You should definitely attend that. Also, I know that some graduates from our engineering department will be attending the career fair as well. I'm sure we could arrange for you to talk with them. You could ask them what their jobs are like.

Ada: That would be great. I really want to know how hands-on engineering work is. I wouldn't mind the academic side of engineering, the math and the physics, but I think I'd really enjoy the actual work of engineering – you know, designing and making things. Computer engineering could be really interesting.

Advisor: You might want to try contacting a computer engineering company here in the city, then. In fact, I could help you with that. We could probably arrange a visit for you.

Ada: That would be fantastic. Thank you.

🔊 **2.2**

See script on page 42.

🔊 **2.3**

1 You're considering going to college, aren't you?
2 I like biology, so I really want to be a doctor.
3 You should consider the courses you like and the courses you do well in when choosing a major.
4 I'm considering studying art history.
5 I've always been interested in the way things work.
6 I think I could do that.
7 I wouldn't mind the academic side of biology.
8 ... but I might enjoy the practical side of linguistics.

🔊 **2.4**

Medical student: Hey, Adam. Come in. Sit down. Want something to drink?

Adam: No, thanks, I'm OK.

Medical student: Have you thought about the **medical** courses I suggested? I loved them when I was an undergrad.

Adam: A little. I've done a little research, but I'm having a hard time deciding what I want to do.

Medical student: That's understandable. There's a lot to think about. Is studying medicine the most important consideration for you?

Adam: Yes and no. The most important thing is probably that I do a medical program of some kind, but not necessarily one that involves a lot of study.

Medical student: OK.

Adam: Getting a **secure** job after I finish my program is important, though, and I really want to help people.

Medical student: What about location? Do you care about where you study?

Adam: Not really. That's probably the least important factor.

Medical student: OK, good. Well, I think we're getting somewhere. You get better grades than I ever did; you should consider studying to become a doctor.

Adam: I'm not sure about that.

Medical student: Really? Why not?

Adam: Well, I guess another one of my criteria is that the job is very **practical**.

Medical student: Sorry, but I have to disagree. I think being a doctor is a very practical job!

Adam: Yes, but I'd rather not have to study for so many years.

Medical student: Maybe you should consider becoming an emergency room nurse.

Adam: I've looked into that.

Medical student: You don't sound too interested in that idea. What else are you considering?

Adam: It depends. I'm not sure what I can apply for. There are a few programs where you can study to become an emergency medical technician – an EMT. They're the people who work on ambulances, assessing patients' conditions, performing emergency procedures, like applying **manual** pressure on someone's wounds after an accident. It also requires some **technical** knowledge of ambulance equipment. It's **professional** and practical.

Medical student: That's a tough job. Exciting, but tough, and very **physical**.

Adam: Yes, but it seems like a great way to really help people when they need it.

Medical student: So, what's the difference between the two programs?

Adam: The EMT program is very practical. When you work in an ambulance, you need a lot of practical skills to help people. You have to be very independent and confident to make decisions on your own, and of course there's the driver training too!

Medical student: OK, I see your point.

Adam: The emergency room nursing program is also practical, but it includes more theoretical work. Especially when you study the core subjects – learning about the human body and about medicine, and so on. It would involve a lot more **complex** study. You have to work closely with hospital staff. It's a degree program.

Medical student: And the EMT program?

Adam: It's a certificate program. So, it would take a lot less time, and I'd be able to start work quickly. It would be great to actually work after so much study. I've been studying my whole life. I'm ready to *do* something, have some adventures, so I'm not too sure about nursing.

Medical student: Yes, I can see that. Continuing on for more schooling like me isn't for everyone. It may not be the ideal program.

Adam: EMTs need in-depth understanding of how to deal with emergencies, and they need the ability to make quick decisions.

Medical student: I think you'd be good at it.

Adam: And if I wanted to continue my training, after working as a basic EMT, I could study to become an EMT specialist. That's another certificate program.

Medical student: But wouldn't you rather study to be a nurse? I imagine the pay would be better.

Adam: You're probably right, but I don't think it's for me.

Medical student: Why don't you get some more information about EMT programs, then, and find out which schools offer that certification.

Adam: That's a great idea.

Medical student: I guess you've made a decision, then. You're going to not follow in my footsteps and instead you'll apply for EMT training.

Adam: I think that's really what I want to do.

🔊 **2.5**

A: I think the most important factor is probably financial need.

B: I'm not sure about that. What if we say that financial need is number two?

C: So, what's number one?

B: I feel it's important to really focus on the applicants' potential contribution to society.

C: I think that's right. Why don't we rank the proposed courses of study according to their contribution to society?

A: OK, I can see your point, but why don't we just say that the interview is number one and financial need is number two?

C/D OK.

B: Wait a minute. I don't agree with that at all. Academic ability is much more important. What if we say that GPA, or grade point average, is the most important factor?

A: I think the rest of us are in agreement about the most important factors.

D: Well, I think the least important thing is the student's written application.

C: Sorry, I don't think I agree. They need to be able to write well.

B: Wait! Have you considered looking at the applicant's family situation?

🔊 **2.6**

1 **A:** Students need to be good at both writing and speaking.

  B: I see. That's understandable.

2 **A:** Hotel workers are important, but emergency medical technicians save lives.

  B: OK, I see your point.

3 **A:** The Chinese language is becoming more important all the time.

  B: You might be right about that.

4 A: Why don't we say emergency medical technicians have the most important job?

B: OK, I think we all can agree with that.

5 A: Do we all agree that financial need is the most important factor?

B: Yes. We've made a decision.

6 A: Can we agree that grade point average is the most important factor?

B: I think we've come to an agreement.

🔊 2.7

Instructor: Hi, and welcome to Western University! Now, you all come from different countries and educational backgrounds, so I'm going to explain some important terms that you need to understand before you sign up for your classes. First of all: credits. Every class carries a certain number of credits. Most classes count for three credits, but some count for two, or four. In order to graduate you'll need to take about 120 credits in total, over four years. For most people, that will translate to between 12 and 15 credits per semester.

Student 1: I'm sorry, can you please say that again? How many credits do we need to take per semester?

Instructor: Most people take between 12 and 15 credits per semester.

Student 2: May I ask a question?

Instructor: Of course!

Student 2: Somebody told me that a three-credit class means three hours of class a week. Is that correct?

Instructor: Yes, that's more or less correct.

Student 2: So in other words, if I'm taking 15 credits, that's about 15 hours of class?

Instructor: Correct. And remember … you can sometimes get credit for work you have done outside college.

Student 1: Can you give us an example?

Instructor: For example, if you have taken an honors-level class in high school.

Student 1: I see …

Student 3: Could I ask about grades? What system do you use?

Instructor: We use a letter system. *A* is the highest grade. An *A* is 90% or higher. A *B* is 80 to 89% percent. A *C* is 70 to 79%. And a D is 65 to 69%. At this school, you need a *C* or better to pass a class. Some teachers do it differently, but that's the most common system.

Student 4: Can you explain the term *GPA*? I hear it a lot but I don't know what it means.

Instructor: *GPA* stands for Grade Point Average. You get four points for an *A*, three points for a *B*, two points for a *C*, and one point for a *D*. Your GPA is the average of all of your points.

Student 4: Thank you.

UNIT 3

 Corporate Wellness

Donna Sharples: My entire life my weight has been an issue. It's been an up-and-down battle.

Elaine Quijano (reporter): Less than two years ago 46-year-old Donna Sharples weighed 275 pounds and suffered from some serious health problems. But for this New Jersey businesswoman, the spark to better health came from her employer, the PHH Corporation. It pays workers up to $1,000 a year to make measurable improvements to their health.

Donna Sharples: I didn't think I'd gain any other benefit out of it, but the chance to earn extra cash was a motivating factor for me, absolutely.

Elaine Quijano: It's called incentive-based health care.

Adele Barbato: It is a win-win.

Elaine Quijano: Chief Human Resources Officer Adele Barbato says the program benefits the workers and the company. As employees get healthier, medical costs go down.

Adele Barbato: So we have less claims costs. We have less sick time, higher productivity, more engaged employees because they're feeling good about taking control of their wellness.

Elaine Quijano: And it really works. For every dollar a company spends on a corporate wellness program, there is a three- to six-dollar return on investment. At this company, the path to wellness starts with a few simple steps, literally.

Donna Sharples: Here's my pedometer.

Elaine Quijano: Everyone in the program gets a pedometer like this one, and every step is counted. The more you walk, the more money you get.

Donna Sharples: In the beginning, I was lucky if I could walk for five minutes straight on a treadmill, honestly, when I first started coming up here. But I just stuck with it and each day tried to add a little more time to it and increased it as much as I could.

Elaine Quijano: Keeping track of your progress is simple. Just plug the pedometer into your PC.

Donna Sharples: To date I've taken four million, thirteen thousand, eight hundred steps.

Elaine Quijano: Employees can also earn credit for being active in other ways, like this cardio class at the on-site gym, in the middle of the work day. And the focus on wellness extends to the cafeteria, which offers fresh, healthy choices. For Donna Sharples, the program has done much more than earn her extra cash and make her healthier. It's transformed her in a more fundamental way, one step at a time. Elaine Quijano, CBS News, New York.

Teacher: Throughout history, there have been many pandemics around the world: measles, malaria, cholera, the flu. So how does a common disease turn from an **outbreak** into a pandemic? Any ideas?

Student 1: People's general health and how close they live to each other can be major **factors** in the spread of disease, can't they?

Student 2: Yeah, so governments need to make sure people are in good health and live in good conditions to stop diseases from spreading.

Teacher: Well, that's a good idea, but there's a limit to what governments can do, especially in times of economic difficulty.

Student 2: And governments don't always have the power to say exactly how everyone should live.

Teacher: So what factors do you think would make a country at a high risk for a pandemic?

Student 3: Well, countries with large populations are probably at risk, especially where large numbers of people live close together.

Student 1: And countries where a lot of international travelers pass through, like the U.K. and other countries in dark and medium blue on the map.

Teacher: That's right. The countries most at risk of a pandemic these days are wealthier countries like the U.K., South Korea, the Netherlands, and Germany. What do those countries have in common?

Student 2: They're not all large countries, but they do all have large cities with big populations.

Student 1: And they're all places where a lot of international travelers might go. They have a lot of airports and potentially thousands of people coming in every day, from all over the world.

Teacher: Correct. If you look at those countries in light blue, they're at a medium or low risk for a pandemic because they have less dense populations, less international travel, fewer borders, etc. OK, so imagine you're an advisor to your government. You want to protect your country from a pandemic. What should you do?

Student 1: You should give everyone a vaccine.

Teacher: A vaccine. OK, good idea. Can anyone explain what that is?

Student 2: It's a kind of medicine, isn't it?

Teacher: Yes, sort of. Most medicines are given to patients after they have the illness, to help them **recover**, but a vaccine is different. A vaccine provides disease **prevention**. If people get the flu vaccine, they often don't become **infected**. So if we wanted to avoid pandemics, then governments would need to implement vaccination programs for common diseases, wouldn't they?

Student 3: The government should force everyone to have vaccines. They should give a vaccine to people as soon as an outbreak **occurs** because prevention is generally much easier than **treatment**. When governments focus on the prevention of disease, pandemics become very rare.

Student 2: I'm not sure I agree. The trouble is, organisms that cause disease, like bacteria or viruses, change every year. So a vaccine that worked really well last year may not be effective this year.

Student 1: There's another thing to consider too; a lot of people don't want to have a vaccine that might not work. The government can't force people to get a vaccine, can it?

Teacher: Well, I don't think any governments do, but in the event of a pandemic, they definitely encourage people to get it, and a lot of people do. People don't want to **contract** a disease, do they? So other than vaccination, what other ways are there of stopping the spread of disease?

Student 1: International travel is a big risk to a disease spreading quickly. We shouldn't allow people with diseases into the country.

Student 3: I'm not sure I agree. The trouble is most people spread diseases before they even know they have them.

Student 2: And there's another problem. How could people prove whether or not they have diseases? It would be impossible to set up a system for checking it.

Student 1: During a pandemic, we should stop all flights from countries that are affected, shouldn't we? If we don't let people into the country, then the disease won't get here.

Student 2: But there's another side to that argument. People travel all the time for business. It would have a terrible effect on the economy, wouldn't it?

Student 3: But also, in most countries, people who live near the border travel back and forth, sometimes every day. If countries stopped people from traveling, a lot of people could lose their jobs. It could also separate families.

Teacher: Well, those are some really interesting views from all of you. Can anyone think of some simpler suggestions for decreasing the risk of pandemics, then? Perhaps not as large scale as closing down country borders?

Student 1: Well, people who have the flu should stay home from school or from work, shouldn't they?

1 A lot of people don't want to have a vaccine that might not work. The government can't force people to get a vaccine, can it?

2 During a pandemic, we should stop all flights from countries that are affected, shouldn't we?

3 People travel all the time for business. It would have a terrible effect on the economy, wouldn't it?

🔊 3.3

1 So this is a very serious disease, isn't it?

2 So this is a very serious disease, isn't it?

3 It's a kind of medicine, isn't it?

4 Governments need to implement vaccination programs for common diseases, don't they?

5 The government can't force people to get a vaccine, can it?

6 People don't want to contract a disease, do they?

7 During a pandemic, we should stop all flights from countries that are affected, shouldn't we?

8 People who have the flu should stay home from school or from work, shouldn't they?

🔊 3.4

Host: Flu season is here, but experts and the public are divided on the subject of vaccination. Those in favor of the flu vaccine say that it may help you avoid getting sick and may also help stop the spread of the disease. They point out that this may save lives. Those experts against the flu vaccine argue that there is no proof that it works. Some go so far as to say that it may be unsafe because it is produced very quickly, though there is no evidence to support this claim.

The fact is that there is no research or **clinical** evidence to show that either side is correct. As the debate continues, statistics show that only about 30% of us choose to get the flu vaccine each year.

🔊 3.5

Host: Since the news that this year's flu vaccine is ready, the government has advised that the old, young, and people with medical problems be vaccinated. However, not everyone thinks vaccination is a good idea. According to the Centers for Disease Control and Prevention, less than 50% of those eligible to get the flu vaccine – most people except for the very young and very old – got the flu vaccine as a **precaution** last year. That means over 50% did not get vaccinated. Of that 50%, some are actively against the flu vaccine.

In today's debate, we'll begin with flu expert Dr. Sandra Smith, who is in favor of flu vaccination. After that, we'll hear from alternative medicine practitioner Mr. Mark Li, who is against flu vaccination.

Dr. Smith will now begin. Dr. Smith?

Dr. Smith: Thank you. Well, influenza, or the flu, is a respiratory disease that can make you feel extremely sick. Most people who get the flu recover after several days. While they may feel terrible, there are usually no long-lasting problems. However, the flu can cause severe illness or worse for a small percentage of the people who get it. It may not sound like a lot, but actually this is hundreds of thousands of people around the world each year. It can be especially serious for the very old and the very young. Obviously, we want to do everything in our power to stop the infection from spreading. This brings us to vaccination. When people get vaccinated, less flu can spread through the population.

Vaccines have saved millions of lives. They're a proven method of disease prevention. Scientists have been developing flu vaccines from the 1930s up to today, so we have a lot of experience with them. **Researchers** make new flu vaccines every year based on the previous year's flu virus. The World Health Organization recommends that children between the ages of six months and five years, people over 65, pregnant women, and anyone who already has a serious illness get the flu vaccine. They also recommend vaccinations for health-care workers.

To finish up, let me say this: I'm a flu specialist. I research the virus and work closely with flu patients all the time, so I'm constantly around the virus. I've gotten the vaccine. All of my colleagues have gotten the vaccine. None of us have caught the flu. If we hadn't gotten the vaccine, we could have caught the flu each year. There's no guarantee that vaccination will prevent you from getting the flu, but it won't hurt you, and there's a chance it could save your life. How would you feel if someone in your family did not get the vaccine and then became really sick?

Host: We'll now have the statement against vaccination from Mr. Mark Li.

Mr. Li: Thank you and thank you, Dr. Smith. Let me start by saying that I'm not against all vaccines. Dr. Smith is absolutely right that many vaccines work very well and that millions of lives have been saved by vaccination. There's plenty of good **scientific data** that **proves** that. If scientists hadn't developed the polio vaccine, the world would be very different today. But let me ask you this: has the flu vaccine been properly tested? Have there been proper clinical **trials** to prove that it works, that it stops infection? Does it really provide prevention of the disease?

For most medicines, the government makes sure that proper tests are carried out, but this isn't the case with the flu vaccine. There isn't one single scientific study that proves that this year's flu vaccine works. The packaging on this flu vaccine clearly states that "No **controlled** trials have been performed that demonstrate that this vaccine causes a reduction in influenza." It's here in black and white.

If it says on the package that there's no proof that it's an effective prevention, why are we using it? Yes, vaccination can be good, but flu vaccination is just a big experiment, and it may actually be doing more harm than good. If it were proven, then I would consider it.

Host: Thank you, Mr. Li. Dr. Smith, do you have anything to add?

Dr. Smith: Thank you. You have some interesting points, Mr. Li. It's true that when the flu emerges every year, it's a bit different than the year before. When making a vaccine, researchers have to try to figure out how the flu is going to change and adjust it to the new virus. If we waited until the new virus emerges, it would be too late.

So while Mr. Li is right – we don't do clinical trials of the flu vaccine in the way that we do trials for other medicines – that doesn't mean we aren't scientific in our methods. I'd definitely like to challenge the idea that there's no scientific basis for our work. I disagree with Mr. Li on that point. Let me tell you more about my work in that area.

We can prove in the laboratory that vaccines can reduce the risk of getting a disease, generally. What we don't know is exactly how this year's flu virus will change, but we can use our experience to make a prediction. As for the question of the vaccine being dangerous: it doesn't contain a live virus, so you definitely can't get the flu from the vaccine. If people are vaccinated and then happen to become sick, that doesn't logically mean the vaccine caused the illness. They were most likely around the virus before they were vaccinated.

Mr. Li: Well, I'm sure Dr. Smith is a very good doctor, but I think the flu vaccine package I mentioned earlier is clear. It's obvious that the vaccine hasn't been properly tested.

The other big concern, of course, is safety. A lot of us believe that the vaccine actually causes people to get sick rather than making them well – so she and I disagree on that point. I'm talking about side effects. Some people have gotten really sick after being vaccinated. This can be anything from headaches to stomach problems. Do you really want to use a medication that might make you sick? Supposing you gave your kids the vaccine and it made them worse

rather than better? Some people also believe that the vaccine may give you the flu rather than stopping you from catching it. I've had patients who were healthy, then got the flu vaccine and got sick. Medicines shouldn't make us sick. That's why I'm against the flu vaccine, and that's why I don't think anyone at all should have it.

Host: Thank you both.

 3.6

1 Affordable health care is an issue for poor people all over the world, and not just in developing countries. In his book, *Pathologies of Power*, published by University of California Press in 2003, Dr. Paul Farmer points out that poor people in some prosperous American cities have a lower life expectancy than people in China or India.

2 Heart disease is a leading cause of death in the United States. According to statistics from the Centers for Disease Control and Prevention, more than 600,000 Americans die of heart disease each year. That's one in every four deaths in this country.

3 Doctors are making progress in fighting cancer. A 2016 report by Rebecca Siegel and her colleagues at the American Cancer Society found that the death rate from cancer has dropped by 23% since 1991.

UNIT 4

▶ Cloning Endangered Species

Reporter: They are called bantengs, and although one of the week-old calves just died, the fact that they were born at all could put scientists one step closer to saving some endangered species. The animals were cloned from the frozen skin cells of a banteng which died 23 years ago.

Man: I'm rather still astounded by the fact that you can take the nucleus of a cell and produce a living animal.

Reporter: It's called *nuclear cell transfer*, injecting the banteng's genetic material into the egg of a living cow. It's been done before with an endangered animal called a gaur. It died in just two days. The banteng was euthanized after developing complications from the cloning. While the news of the birth is astonishing, it also worries some conservationists.

Conservationist: If you don't deal with protecting habitat and dealing with all the root causes of endangerment, it doesn't matter how many animals you are able to produce in the lab and try to sort of fling back into the wild, they're going to face the same fate as their wild counterparts.

Reporter: The scientists at Advanced Cell Technology in Massachusetts, where both the banteng and gaur were cloned, agree to some extent.

Scientist: However, it doesn't make much sense to preserve the habitat if you don't have any animals to preserve.

Reporter: If you're wondering, "Can this technology be used to clone extinct animals like the mammoth," hold on. Since cloning needs preserved animal tissue, bringing back the dinosaurs remains the stuff of science fiction, for now.

🔊 4.1

Planet Earth is dynamic and always changing. Just 10,000 years ago, about half of the planet was covered in ice, but before that period, the Earth had been very steamy and warm, with vast forests and large bodies of water. It may surprise you that oceans had covered the whole planet until about 2.5 billion years ago, when land formed above sea level. As you can see, the Earth has experienced quite a lot of environmental change.

Today only about 10% of the planet is covered in ice, as the Earth has been warming since the last ice age. Part of this environmental change is due to natural, rather than human, causes.

Sometimes, natural forces can destroy the environment. In 1991, a volcano in the Philippines erupted and killed many people and animals. It destroyed around 300 square miles of farmland and a huge area of forest. It also caused severe floods when rivers were blocked with volcanic ash.

However, humans are also responsible for a lot of habitat destruction. There were originally more than 6 million square miles of rainforest worldwide. Less than three and a half million remain today, and deforestation is occurring at a rate of approximately 1,722,225 square feet per year. In Europe, only about 15% of land hasn't been **modified** by humans.

In some places, **habitats** haven't been destroyed, but they have been broken into parts, for example, separated by roads. This is called fragmentation. If animals are used to moving around throughout the year and a road is built through the middle of their habitat, fragmentation can cause serious problems.

Humans haven't only affected the land and its animals; they have also affected the sea. Pollution from **coastal** cities has damaged the ocean environment and destroyed the habitat of fish and other sea life.

Habitat destruction hasn't been bad news for all animals. In fact, some species have **adapted** extremely well to living closely with people and benefit from living near them.

In Africa and Asia, monkeys live in cities alongside people and **exploit** the human environment by stealing food or eating things that humans have thrown away. In Singapore, the 1,500 wild monkeys that live in and around the city have become a tourist attraction. In North America, coyotes have wandered into urban areas, even big cities like San Francisco and Chicago. Coyotes have learned to cross busy roads safely to find places to live in the city without being noticed. They survive by eating a wide variety of things, such as gophers, squirrels, and rabbits, but not everyone welcomes the coyotes. They sometimes eat people's dogs and cats and might attack pet owners if they try to defend their dogs or cats. Likewise, police in India recently spotted several young leopards in the streets of Mumbai. The leopards had moved into the city from the nearby forests. One expert said that the surprising thing was that leopards had been in the city for a long time, but people rarely saw them. Leopards are very secretive, and they prefer not to be seen.

One other animal that is as at home in both the city and in the countryside is the raccoon. In fact, raccoons are so at home in the city that the number of city raccoons has increased. Raccoons have different diets depending on their environment. Common foods include fruit, plants, nuts, and rodents. Raccoons living in the city eat garbage.

We tend to think of human activity as always having a negative **impact** on the environment. However, some people feel that we can have a positive impact, too.

Conservation means trying to save habitats. Ecotourism is an approach to travel and vacations where people visit natural areas such as rainforests, except rather than destroy the environment, they help preserve it. Visitors to the La Selva Amazon Eco Lodge in Ecuador watch and learn about local wildlife, visit tribes who live in the forest, and stay in an environmentally friendly hotel. Their presence doesn't damage the local environment, and most guests leave the hotel as conservationists. When they experience the beauty of nature firsthand, they feel strongly that they want to protect and preserve it.

Not everyone feels that ecotourism is actually helping the environment. Tourists who travel long distances by airplane create pollution, as do resorts, which use local resources such as fresh water and produce **waste** that creates pollution in the local environment.

🔊 4.2

See script on page 88.

🔊 4.3

Before she wrote her influential book *Silent Spring* in 1962, Rachel Carson had spent years working for the U.S. government at environmental agencies like the U.S. Bureau of Fisheries and the U.S. Fish and Wildlife Service. During her time there, she did her own personal research and writing. By 1955, Carson had already published several books on environmental research when she began to do research full-time. One subject that she was particularly interested in was the effects of pesticides on the environment and on human health. During World War II, the government used the pesticide DDT to protect people against diseases caused by pests. After the war, farmers sprayed large amounts of DDT into the air to protect their crops. Carson had heard that the chemical was making people sick with cancer and was causing other animals to die, so she decided to do scientific research on the subject and publish it as a book to warn people about the risks. After Carson released *Silent Spring*, the pesticide industry attacked her for her research. However, the U.S. government responded by banning the use of DDT in the United States. Soon her book was translated into several languages and was published around the world.

🔊 4.4

The topic of my talk is the decline and destruction of the world's deserts. First, I'm going to talk about the desert environment and wildlife. Then we'll look at the threats to this environment. Finally, we'll talk about what is being done to save the world's deserts.

Let's begin by looking at some background information from the United Nations Environment Programme. The United Nations reports in *Global Deserts Outlook* that the Earth's deserts cover about 13 million square miles, or about 25% of the Earth's surface. Deserts are home to 560 million people, or about 8% of the world's population, but as I'll explain, people all over the world rely on things that come from this environment.

Humans have learned to exploit the resources of the desert for survival and profit by adapting their behavior, culture, and technology to this **harsh** environment. To give you an example, tribes such as the Topnaar in southwestern Africa are known for their ability to survive in deserts due to their use of local plants and animals for food, medicine, and clothing. They have an understanding of the natural world. The Bedouins, who live from North Africa to the Syrian deserts, are skilled at using animals to provide transportation, food, and clothing and also at growing basic foods around desert rivers. The Topnaar and the Bedouins are just two examples of people who live in and rely on the desert environment for the things they need. However, city dwellers benefit from the desert, too.

Certain **minerals** are found in deserts, which provide a large portion of the world's **diamonds**, as well as **copper**, gold, and other metals. Deserts are a major source of oil and **natural gas**, too. These desert products are used by industries and people all over the world every day. Until these natural resources were discovered, of course, changes to desert habitats had not really affected people very much. But what I'm saying is that nowadays, even though most people may not live in a desert, we actually are all affected by these kinds of environmental changes, even if we live in cities. Agricultural products are also grown in deserts and exported around the world. Because their climates are warm and their land tends to be inexpensive, desert countries are able to grow and sell food all year. A good example of this is Egyptian cotton. New methods of irrigation are being developed so that desert agricultural systems can use water more efficiently. So we can see that deserts are important, not only for the people who live in them, but for everyone who uses products that come from a desert environment. That's all I have to say on that point.

Moving on to the typical desert environment. In summer, the ground surface temperature in most deserts reaches 175 degrees Fahrenheit (80 degrees Celsius), and there is very little rain. Despite these harsh conditions, a wide variety of plants and animals live in and are supported by this environment. For example, there are reportedly over 2,200 different plant species in the desert regions of Saudi Arabia, based on research from King Saud University.

Small plants are especially important in a desert environment because they hold the soil in place, which allows larger plants to grow. Acacia trees can grow well in extremely hot, dry conditions, but its seeds need stable soil to begin growing. Smaller plants, therefore, help the larger ones, and in this way, all desert plants help hold the dry soil in place, which helps reduce dust storms.

Deserts are also an important animal habitat. One of the best known desert animals in the Arabian Peninsula is the Arabian oryx, which weighs about 150 pounds (68 kilograms) and is about three feet tall – that's almost a meter. It rests during the heat of the day and searches for food and water when temperatures are cooler. Experts say that the oryx can sense rain and move towards it.

These examples show that the desert is an ecosystem that supports a variety of important plant and animal life. The problem is that human activity is affecting modern deserts. According to the United Nations, traditional ways of life are changing as human activities such as cattle ranching, farming, and large-scale tourism grow. The process of bringing water into the desert to grow plants is making the soil too salty. The construction of dams for power generation and water supply and an increase in **mining** have also begun to have a greater impact on the desert. Owing to the destruction of desert plants, dust storms are more common, and desert animals, therefore, have less food to eat. Data from the United Nations shows that every year, nearly 2% of healthy desert disappears. Today, more than 50% of the world's desert habitats are **wilderness** areas, but by 2050, it may be as low as 31%.

If we lose the world's deserts, we lose everything I spoke about in the first part of my talk. The Topnaar and Bedouin way of life will certainly disappear, but what does this mean for the rest of the world? Well, everyone on Earth will experience an increase of dust and dirt in the air as desert plants die. If desert soil becomes too salty to grow plants, we'll also lose a valuable source of food, and I'm talking about foods that we all eat. If we allow deserts to be destroyed, life all over Earth will change. To put it another way, we will all be affected. Now, the big question is, what is being done about the destruction of deserts?

The United Nations Environment Programme offers two main solutions. First, we can begin to manage desert resources carefully, instead of abusing them. This means using the desert for things we need, as well as not damaging it further. It would mean carefully controlling the way we use water. Secondly, we can apply technological solutions. The UN gives the example of using the latest computer technology to help forecast how climate change will affect deserts and using that information to prepare for these changes. We can also make better use of two resources freely available in the desert: the wind and the sun. These can be used to provide clean energy on a fairly small scale within existing desert cities. According to the blog *A Smarter Planet*, scientists in Saudi Arabia are already using solar energy to produce fresh water in the desert for agricultural use.

To summarize, deserts are not only important to the people who live in them, but to plants, animals, and people everywhere, from the Bedouin tribes to city dwellers. Human activity is causing the destruction of desert habitats, but there are ways in which we can help stop this.

🔊 4.5

Anchor: Are you a procrastinator? Do you often put off doing your work, your homework, or your assignments for your classes? Well, you are not alone. A recent survey of 1,300 high school and college students found that approximately 87% of high school and college students regularly avoid or postpone schoolwork. Almost half of the students that procrastinate – 45% – said that procrastination often has a bad effect on their grades.

The report found that male and female students procrastinate for slightly different reasons. Male students are more likely to say that they don't like doing schoolwork and they would rather be doing something else. Female students are more likely to say they feel overwhelmed – they have so much to do that they don't know where to start.

So what are students doing instead of studying? The answer is not a surprise. For both males and females, the most common ways of avoiding schoolwork were watching movies or TV and using social media.

Here in our studio we have Mercedes Kaufman, who is a student advisor at Western University. Mercedes, does any of this information surprise you?

Kaufman: No. Procrastination is a huge problem among college students, both male and female – particularly younger students who are coming straight from high school.

Anchor: And do you think that social media has an effect on this?

Kaufman: Yes, I think so. There are so many distractions, and it's so easy to spend an hour playing a game on your phone or looking at social media. Students really need to learn how to manage their time.

Anchor: Can you give us an example of some strategies that students could use?

Kaufman: Well, we train students to organize their time by using planners and to-do lists. We show them how to divide up the work they have to do and see how they can do things a bit at a time. We also teach them to plan their work at the time of day when they are likely to be most productive.

Anchor: Thank you, Mercedes. Now we'd like to hear from our listeners. What strategies do you use to avoid procrastinating? Give us a call at 905 …

UNIT 5

▶ The Skyscraper

New York City may have made them famous, but skyscrapers were born in Chicago, Illinois. A terrible fire in 1871 made it possible for architects to experiment with new building techniques that would allow them to make buildings taller than ever before. These stately brown stone buildings are some of the world's first skyscrapers.

Louis Sullivan, known as the father of the skyscraper, lived and worked in Chicago. This is his Auditorium Building on Michigan Avenue, completed in 1889. Sullivan believed that the new social and economic strength of the United States required a new architecture. And his idea that tall buildings represent power is still popular 125 years later.

Sullivan described the skyscraper as the perfect symbol of the proud spirit of the American man. But it was really the symbol of the proud American businessman. By 1920, there were over 300,000 corporations in the United States, serving 100 million consumers in an enormous single market – it was the biggest, most powerful economy the world had ever seen.

Above all, skyscrapers represented American corporate success. They changed the appearance of American cities. The skylines of New York and Chicago looked like bar charts or graphs, with the tallest buildings representing the richest, most powerful companies. And the same is still true in cities around the world today – from Dubai to Shanghai, from Seoul to Kuala Lumpur.

🔊 **5.1**

Alan: Khalid, we need to talk about that warehouse the company plans to **obtain** in Westside.

Khalid: OK. I've just seen the pictures. I think there's a lot of **potential** there.

Alan: Really? I'm afraid we might be biting off more than we can chew.

Khalid: Really? Why?

Alan: First, the problem is the Westside area itself. Thirty years ago, it was a thriving industrial neighborhood with a lot of businesses. Now, it's a half-empty wasteland. It's ugly. There are lots of abandoned buildings, and the area isn't really used for anything. No one wants to go there. Second, the warehouse we're looking at is in terrible condition. It was abandoned about 20 years ago. It's beginning to sink into the ground, and it's falling apart – we would need to do some serious work to bring the building back to good condition Acquiring such an old building could be a huge mistake.

Khalid: Really? I think the project is going to be a great success. In fact, I think it's a potential goldmine.

Alan: Um, OK. Could you expand on that?

Khalid: There's been a lot of activity in Westside recently. There is development and restoration going on nearby, and I think it's really going to **transform** the area. Westside is becoming popular with people who work in the financial district, which is close by. Rent is still low there, and a new restaurant opens almost every week. I **anticipate** the neighborhood becoming really trendy. No one has spent much money there in the past 20 years, but **investment** in the area has increased in the past year. We're going to see a lot more improvement as well.

Alan: That may be true, but that building is more like a prison than a potential shopping mall. People would never want to go shopping there. I think the first thing we'd need to do would be tear it down, and that would cost us a lot of money.

Khalid: Have you considered doing work on the building instead of tearing it down? It has some beautiful original **features**.

Alan: It looks like it's probably going to **collapse**!

Khalid: I'm not sure it's that bad. I think the original building has a lot of potential.

Alan: I think we really want to transform the area with something modern. Why not just start over and build a new building?

Khalid: If we designed it properly, we could maintain the old architectural features, such as the red bricks and the stone. Those construction materials would better match the style of some of the other buildings around it. It would reflect the character of the area. We are going to give the old building a new lease on life.

Alan: Maybe, but I think it would be better to transform the area with an architectural landmark, something new and **contemporary**. It would be more of a transformation if we built a modern building made of materials like steel and glass.

Khalid: Couldn't we do both? We'll maintain more of a connection to the past if we include the old building as part of the new one. We could rebuild the warehouse using red bricks similar to those in the original structure and construct a new glass and steel extension – adding on to the building rather than building a whole new building. It would also create more floor space that could be used for retail space. We'd have enough room for at least two or three stores there.

Alan: I hadn't thought of doing it that way.

Khalid: Another option to consider would be putting stores on the ground floor and apartments or offices above. If we added a floor or two to the top of the building, we could definitely use glass and steel for that.

Alan: Would they be luxury apartments?

Khalid: Maybe. We could have a modern, urban, or city-like design using the old architectural materials and features.

Alan: Such as?

Khalid: We could keep some of the original features as they are, such as the long and heavy pieces of wood used to support the ceilings and the inside of the red brick supporting walls that help support the roof. They would then become a decorative feature.

Alan: So not traditional apartments at all, then?

Khalid: No, not at all. Very modern.

Alan: It's an expensive plan, and not everyone will like it.

Khalid: We wouldn't be the first to do this sort of thing, though. We can look at some other examples around the city where the same thing has been done successfully, if you're interested in the idea.

Alan: If we make that the first phase of our planning process, we can make a better decision about how to balance the traditional and modern features of the project before we go on to the design and building phases.

Khalid: There's probably a Westside neighborhood association or business association. We could meet with them and get their views.

Alan: You're right. We really should speak to some businesspeople in the area and arrange to take a better look at the building.

Khalid: Let's do it.

🔊 **5.2**

See script on page 109.

🔊 **5.3**

Jamal: Maria, John. Thanks for taking the time to meet with us.

Maria and John: No problem. / My pleasure.

Jamal: We have the first set of plans, and we think you'll be really pleased with what we've put together. After discussing a lot of options, we now anticipate building a single eight-story apartment building.

Tom: You can see from the pictures here that we are certainly going to fit this into the area by using part of the wasteland, the large area of land that hasn't been developed behind the current housing area.

Jamal: One of the biggest benefits of this plan is that it will create housing for as many as 200 people.

Maria: I can't quite tell from the drawing ... what materials are you going to use?

Tom: The outside is made of glass and steel.

John: And what's the cost of this plan?

Jamal: Around eight million dollars.

Maria: Eight million? Wow. The plan is definitely **ambitious**!

Jamal: Yes, we're aware that it's over the construction budget of 7.5 million, but we are going to review the budget in light of some of our suggestions.

Maria: Well, I have to say, we weren't expecting the building to be so tall.

John: Exactly. The **existing** buildings in the neighborhood are no higher than two stories, and you've placed the new building very close to them. I'm **concerned** about the other buildings on the site. The plan would block daylight for existing homes. We're probably going to get a lot of complaints from the current residents.

Jamal: We could consider using reflective glass instead, then. You know, like a mirror. It's used in big cities to give a feeling of open sky.

Maria: That's a great idea, but I'm not sure it addresses the main problem. The real issue here is the height of the building. I strongly recommend that you reconsider this. After all, we originally suggested housing for about 100 people.

Tom: Yes, we've doubled that.

Maria: OK. Would you mind telling us a bit more about why you decided that?

Jamal: Well, our thinking was that this would increase your company's income from the building because you could sell or rent more apartments.

John: We thought that might be an option at first, too, but now we realize it won't work. We have to think about the houses that are already in the area. We really need to consider how the new building will contribute to the look of the area – that is, how it will fit in with the other buildings.

Tom: When you say "fit in," do you mean we should copy the style of existing buildings?

John: No. We don't expect you to copy, but we also don't want to completely transform the feeling of the area either. So by "fit in," I mean that it should look as though it belongs there. Our original suggestion was that the building should reflect the size and materials of the other buildings in the area.

Tom: OK, I see what you mean.

John: I have one other concern. You described the natural area you'd like to build on as "wasteland," but actually, those are woods. The kids who already live in the area play there, and we want to maintain that open, natural area with all the trees. The residents really value having access to nature nearby.

Maria: Exactly.

John: As it stands, this plan with the tall, single building and the loss of the natural space would be very **controversial**. Wouldn't it be better if we used the first design you supplied to identify a few priorities?

Jamal: Yes, that's a good idea.

Maria: OK ... first, we need to think about what will be **appropriate** with the existing houses. What about more smaller, shorter buildings? We could have four two-story buildings and, following our original plan, try to house 100 rather than 200 people. That might be better.

John: And while we like the idea of contemporary design, I'm not sure glass and steel is appropriate. Lots of glass is a great idea, but in my view, the only viable option is to use brick, like the existing buildings.

Tom: OK. So we're talking about four two-storey brick buildings that can house about 25 people each?

John: Right.

Tom: That seems like an obvious solution, but it doesn't address the issue of cost.

John: What do you mean?

Tom: Well, four smaller buildings will cost more than one larger one.

John: Well, I guess we'll have to see the actual costs to discuss that. Are we going to consider three buildings?

Tom: Yes, that's a possibility.

Jamal: And you mentioned having **adequate** green space. We didn't realize children play in those woods. We need to be **sympathetic** to their needs, so we need to find a different solution. How about we position the new buildings near the edge of the woods?

Maria: Yes, that's possible. We can't acquire the land next to our site because it's public property, but we can benefit from being near that open space. The residents would definitely be able to enjoy the views then.

Tom: I like your thinking. I completely agree.

Jamal: OK, so I think we need to go back and start over again.

John: Yes, I think you're right. I'm sorry, I hope we didn't waste your time.

Jamal: Not at all. I think we understand the site a lot better now, and I feel confident we can come up with a good plan over the next two weeks.

🔊 5.4

See script on page 115.

🔊 5.5

See script on page 118.

🔊 5.6

Student 1: Keep up with your course work. In college, there's usually nobody to tell you to study, so it's easy to just put it off. But there are quizzes and tests all the time … and reading … and papers … and you're supposed to do a lot of work on your own outside class. So you really can't wait until the end of the semester to study.

Student 2: When you choose your classes, don't just take classes your friends are taking … or classes that you think are going to be easy. Take a class in a new subject … maybe something that you don't know a lot about. It helps you to explore your interests and get to know the different fields of study that are out there. It might be your favorite class of the whole semester!

Student 3: It's really important to ask questions in class. Usually other people have the same question, so it helps the class. Professors also expect you to participate in group work and discussions, and you usually get a better grade when you do!

Student 4: Get to know your professors. Go see them during office hours when you have questions. It shows that you're interested, and they're usually happy to help you. If you have a good relationship with a professor in your field, you can learn a lot from them. Sometimes you can help them with their research.

UNIT 6

▶ Solar Panels at Home

Barry Mathis: You gotta back up a little bit, whoa.

Thalia Assuras (reporter): Meet Barry and Anita Mathis. Two kids …

Barry Mathis: Give it to Mommy.

Thalia Assuras: Big new house …

Barry Mathis: My favorite feature of the house is the curved staircase.

Thalia Assuras: And a tiny electric bill.

Anita Mathis: It was kind of mind-blowing when I first moved into this house because I would open power bills, and I would just start laughing. Because it just didn't make any sense that you could save this much money on electricity.

Thalia Assuras: It's not that the Mathises are energy sensitive. They have big appliances and, of course, air conditioning. The secret is on the roof. Look closely. Those shiny panels are solar energy pads.

Barry Mathis: You almost have to show people where the tiles are that are solar. If it had big space-invader stuff on top of the house, definitely would have been a problem for me.

Thalia Assuras: I've never done an interview on a roof before, I have to tell you. This is a solar revolution in the making. Solar panels are now relatively small, fit seamlessly into a roof, and shrink energy costs. Are these solar panels going to pay for the energy of this house?

Man: They're going to offset 70% of the consumption of this house.

Thalia Assuras: My bill is 70% less.

Man: Correct.

John Rawlston: As you see, we're still doing a lot of work in here.

Thalia Assuras: Developer John Rawlston has built 150 solar homes in California. All have this unique feature: they can make so much energy, they feed power to the electric company, literally making the meter spin backwards, reducing the bill. How's that possible?

John Rawlston: If you're creating more electricity than you're using, it will spin backwards, and it will actually reduce your total kilowatts.

Thalia Assuras: So I could get zero, couldn't I?

John Rawlston: You could have less than zero.

Thalia Assuras: You know the saying about a home's biggest selling point – it's all about location, location, location. Well, that's a major problem with this concept. Unless you live in a place like California with all this sunshine, it's just not practical. But builders claim that's going to change soon. They say these panels are so efficient they will be usable even in states with short days and less light.

John Rawlston: We are making electricity right now.

Thalia Assuras: Yeah, you can see it right here on the meter.

The state of California covers about half the cost, and local power companies are required to give homeowners credit for the power their house makes.

Barry Mathis: When we're away, we're making money.

Thalia Assuras: But don't think the Mathises spend any time watching their meter.

Barry Mathis: And that's really one of the pretty parts of the whole idea, is that this happens without us knowing anything about it. It's just there.

Thalia Assuras: They just enjoy the house, bask in the easy money, and let the sun do the work. In Roseville, California, I'm Thalia Assuras for *Eye on America*.

🔊 6.1

Reporter: This is Andrew Thompson, reporting from the Spanish island of El Hierro, about 250 miles (400 kilometers) off the coast of Africa. It's pretty far from Madrid, which is about 1,250 miles (2,000 kilometers) away. Today, we're going to talk to two of the 11,000 people who live here, to find out what's so special about the island. First, this is Pedro Rodriguez, who owns a seafood restaurant on the island. Hello, Pedro.

Pedro: Hello, Andrew.

Reporter: So, how long have you lived on El Hierro?

Pedro: I haven't lived here for very long. I came from Madrid about five years ago.

Reporter: Don't you like it here?

Pedro: I love it here! I wish I had come a lot sooner than I did. I spent most of my life in Madrid.

Reporter: City life can be tough. I suppose island life is rather more relaxing.

Pedro: Exactly. El Hierro is my home now.

Reporter: So, what's so great about El Hierro?

Pedro: In the city, everyone hurries everywhere. You are surrounded by traffic, and you never feel like you can really relax. What's more, my career was in banking, which is an especially stressful job.

I love the sound of the sea. I love the peace and quiet, and I feel free here. City life was never like that. When I was living in the city, I worked in banking, as I said. It paid well and I was able to buy my restaurant, but I should have left the city when I was a much younger man.

Reporter: So you love the quiet life on El Hierro, but is there anything else that makes El Hierro special?

Pedro: Well, for one thing, El Hierro is completely energy independent!

Reporter: Energy independent?

Pedro: Yes. In the past, the power on the island was provided by oil. A lot of money was paid to ship 40,000 barrels of oil over from the **mainland** every year. It cost the island over two million dollars a year. Now, all our energy is created right here on the island.

Reporter: And for more about that, we'll now talk to engineer Sofia Martinez.

Sofia: Hello, Andrew.

Reporter: I wonder if you could tell us about the way you **generate** energy here on El Hierro.

Sofia: Well, if you've spent a day or two here, you may have noticed we have a lot of wind.

Reporter: Yes. In fact, it's blowing pretty hard outside right now.

Sofia: Well, for about 3,000 hours, or for about 30% of the year, the wind here blows hard enough to turn wind turbines, which can provide electricity.

Reporter: Does El Hierro rely completely on wind to power the island?

Sofia: No. The island's wind turbines have a **capacity** of about 11 megawatts, about enough to power 3,500 homes, but it's only one **element**. The bigger problem is that the wind doesn't blow all the time, so the power source isn't **consistent**.

Reporter: So you need another energy source on windless days?

Sofia: That was the challenge: to create an energy generation system, or a **network** of systems, that could supply enough energy for the island all the time. And the solution was hydroelectric power.

Reporter: What is hydroelectric power exactly?

Sofia: Hydroelectric power is when energy is converted into another form, such as electricity. The initial source of this energy is from water.

Reporter: But doesn't hydroelectric power require a river and a dam? Isn't El Hierro too small for a river?

Sofia: A river with a dam is the usual way of producing hydroelectric power, but really, all you need is water that can move from a high place to a lower place to get energy from the water.

Reporter: OK ...

Sofia: At the center of El Hierro is a dormant volcano – a volcano that is no longer active. In the middle of the volcano, we built a **reservoir** that holds over 17 million cubic feet (500,000 cubic meters) of water, at a height of 2,297 feet (700 meters) above sea level. So that's our water in a high place.

Reporter: But you don't get much rain here. What happens when all of the water runs out of the reservoir?

Sofia: Well, I mentioned the wind turbines. The wind power and the hydroelectric power are in a network together. When the wind is blowing, energy from the wind turbines pumps water up into the reservoir.

Reporter: So the wind turbines power the pumping station?

Sofia: Right. We also use the wind power for all of our electrical needs, when it blows. Then when the wind stops, we let water run out of the reservoir and through some turbines. The turbines turn generators and we have hydroelectric power we can access.

Reporter: So the water flows in a **cycle** – it's pumped up the hill by the wind, then it's released when it's needed.

Sofia: Yes, that's right. What's more, the system also provides our drinking water and water for use in agriculture.

Reporter: But where does the water come from?

Sofia: We use seawater.

Reporter: But you can't drink saltwater …

Sofia: We have a desalination plant to take the salt out of the seawater so it can be used in agriculture and as drinking water. We're constantly adding new water and taking stored water out of the cycle as we need to use it. In fact, I've just come from the desalination plant, where we're having some problems today. Something isn't working properly, and the replacement parts haven't arrived yet. We're a long way from the mainland, so delivery of anything takes at least a few days. If they don't come soon, we may have to ask people to use less water for a few days.

Reporter: You're a long way from everything out here, aren't you? It must be difficult sometimes.

Sofia: Well, it's a real challenge living here. On the other hand, we all love it. It can be a hard life, but I wouldn't live anywhere else.

🔊 6.2

Reporter: This is Andrew Thompson, reporting from the Spanish island of El Hierro, about 250 miles (400 kilometers) off the coast of Africa. It's pretty far from Madrid, which is nearly 1,250 miles (2,000 kilometers) away. Today, we're going to talk to two of the 11,000 people who live here, to find out what's so special about the island. First, this is Pedro Rodriguez, who owns a seafood restaurant on the island. Hello, Pedro.

Pedro: Hello, Andrew.

Reporter: So, how long have you lived on El Hierro?

Pedro: I haven't lived here for very long. I came from Madrid about five years ago.

Reporter: Don't you like it here?

Pedro: I love it here! I wish I had come a lot sooner than I did. I spent most of my life in Madrid.

Reporter: City life can be tough. I suppose island life is rather more relaxing.

Pedro: Exactly. El Hierro is my home now.

Reporter: So, what's so great about El Hierro?

Pedro: In the city, everyone hurries everywhere. You are surrounded by traffic, and you never feel like you can really relax. What's more, my career was in banking, which is an especially stressful job.
I love the sound of the sea. I love the peace and quiet, and I feel free here. City life was never like that. When I was living in the city, I worked in banking, as I said. It paid well and I was able to buy my restaurant, but I should have left the city when I was a much younger man.

Reporter: So you love the quiet life on El Hierro, but is there anything else that makes El Hierro special?

Pedro: Well, for one thing, El Hierro is completely energy independent!

Reporter: Energy independent?

Pedro: Yes. In the past, the power on the island was provided by oil. A lot of money was paid to ship 40,000 barrels of oil over from the mainland every year. It cost the island over two million dollars a year. Now, all our energy is created right here on the island.

🔊 6.3

Reporter: And for more about that, we'll now talk to engineer Sofia Martinez.

Sofia: Hello, Andrew.

Reporter: I wonder if you could tell us about the way you generate energy here on El Hierro.

Sofia: Well, if you've spent a day or two here, you may have noticed we have a lot of wind.

Reporter: Yes. In fact, it's blowing pretty hard outside right now.

Sofia: Well, for about 3,000 hours, or for about 30% of the year, the wind here blows hard enough to turn wind turbines, which can provide electricity.

Reporter: Does El Hierro rely completely on wind to power the island?

Sofia: No. The island's wind turbines have a capacity of about 11 megawatts, about enough to power 3,500 homes, but it's only one element. The bigger problem is that the wind doesn't blow all the time, so the power source isn't consistent.

Reporter: So you need another energy source on windless days?

Sofia: That was the challenge: to create an energy generation system, or a network of systems, that could supply enough energy for the island all the time. And the solution was hydroelectric power.

Reporter: What is hydroelectric power exactly?

Sofia: Hydroelectric power is when energy is converted into another form, such as electricity. The initial source of this energy is from water.

Reporter: But doesn't hydroelectric power require a river and a dam? Isn't El Hierro too small for a river?

Sofia: A river with a dam is the usual way of producing hydroelectric power, but really, all you need is water that can move from a high place to a lower place to get energy from the water.

Reporter: OK ...

Sofia: At the center of El Hierro is a dormant volcano – a volcano that is no longer active. In the middle of the volcano, we built a reservoir that holds over 17 million cubic feet (500,000 cubic meters) of water, at a height of 2,297 feet (700 meters) above sea level. So that's our water in a high place.

Reporter: But you don't get much rain here. What happens when all of the water runs out of the reservoir?

Sofia: Well, I mentioned the wind turbines. The wind power and the hydroelectric power are in a network together. When the wind is blowing, energy from the wind turbines pumps water up into the reservoir.

Reporter: So the wind turbines power the pumping station?

Sofia: Right. We also use the wind power for all of our electrical needs, when it blows. Then when the wind stops, we let water run out of the reservoir and through some turbines. The turbines turn generators and we have hydroelectric power we can access.

Reporter: So the water flows in a cycle – it's pumped up the hill by the wind, then it's released when it's needed.

Sofia: Yes, that's right. What's more, the system also provides our drinking water and water for use in agriculture.

Reporter: But where does the water come from?

Sofia: We use seawater.

Reporter: But you can't drink saltwater ...

Sofia: We have a desalination plant to take the salt out of the seawater so it can be used in agriculture and as drinking water. We're constantly adding new water and taking stored water out of the cycle as we need to use it. In fact, I've just come from the desalination plant, where we're having some problems today. Something isn't working properly and the replacement parts haven't arrived yet. We're a long way from the mainland, so delivery of anything takes at least a few days. If they don't come soon, we may have to ask people to use less water for a few days.

Reporter: You're a long way from everything out here, aren't you? It must be difficult sometimes.

Sofia: Well, it's a real challenge living here. On the other hand, we all love it. It can be a hard life, but I wouldn't live anywhere else.

🔊 **6.4**

See script on page 132.

🔊 **6.5**

See script on page 132.

🔊 **6.6**

1 In certain states fracking is banned due to its dangerous effects on the environment.

2 Humans, animals, and the environment could all be threatened by the use of nuclear energy.

3 The community refuses to allow the power company to build a new plant by the river.

4 Salt is removed from the water at the desalination plant.

5 We are a completely energy-independent country.

6 I don't think we should use fossil fuels at all anymore.

🔊 **6.7**

Jane: As you all know, there's been a proposal that we should try to reduce our energy **consumption** here in the office, both to save money for the business and to help the environment. The **function** of this meeting today is to get your ideas on how to do this and hopefully to come up with a plan to take forward. Would anyone like to start? What are your views? Yes, Zara.

Zara: Well, if we really want to do something to save on electricity costs long-term, why don't we consider an alternative energy source? We could install some solar panels on the roof. That would generate plenty of environmentally friendly electricity.

Jane: That's not a bad idea. Would anyone like to add to Zara's comments? Allen?

Allen: It's true that we could go for a big solution like solar power generation. Even so, I think we could consider some rather simpler, smaller-scale ideas too, like changing to low-energy lightbulbs. There's a lot of potential to save energy there.

Jane: I think that's a great point, Allen. Abdul, would you like to expand on that?

Abdul: Yes. Allen's lightbulb idea is a really good one. Energy-efficient bulbs aren't hugely expensive to install. In addition, they pay for themselves quickly.

Jane: "Pay for themselves?"

Abdul: They don't use much energy, so they're cheap to run. It means they will soon save us more money than the cost of the new bulbs. Although these energy-efficient bulbs are expensive, we would save enough money in one year to pay for them.

Jane: I see. Do you have any other ideas?

Abdul: Yes. Some of the ideas are very simple: cleaning our dirty windows, for example. As a result of that, we'll allow more natural light in. Furthermore, we can turn off our computer screens when we get up from our desks.

Jane: Yes, Zara.

Zara: We could also consider turning off the air conditioning when it isn't too hot, so we can use less energy.

Jane: Great idea.

Zara: We could get rid of one of our photocopiers, too, as we don't really need two. The current machines use energy even when they're on standby.

Jane: Also a good plan. Now, I'd like to go back to Abdul. Abdul, you said we should consider smaller-scale solutions to our energy consumption here. Are you saying you're against installing a solar energy system?

Abdul: No, I really like that idea because once it's installed, the system will have a low operating cost, and it's an environmentally friendly way to generate electricity, which are two big positive points, but there are other considerations. For example, we'd have to look at the generating capacity of the system. It's very expensive to buy and install, and if it doesn't produce a lot of power, it'll end up costing rather than saving us money, at least for the first few years. The challenge is to choose ways of saving energy that also save money right now.

Allen: Yes, I agree with that. The other real environmental problem we have here in the office is trash. Most of us buy our lunch in plastic containers that have to be thrown away. It's a disgrace. We really should try to reduce the **volume** of trash we create here in the office.

Jane: Sorry, but that's not really what we're discussing right now. We can deal with waste and recycling later. Right now we're talking specifically about energy use.

Allen: Okay, fine. Sorry about that.

Zara: So, we were talking about turning off computer screens and turning off the air conditioning, but I don't think we should forget about installing solar panels, or a solar water heating system.

Jane: But there are some **drawbacks** to that, such as the installation cost, which Abdul mentioned.

Abdul: Right, and there's also the problem of ...

Simon: Can I just say, by the way ...

Jane: Sorry, but could you hold that thought until Abdul has finished, please?

Simon: Sure. Sorry.

Abdul: The fact is, both systems Zara mentioned are technically complex and expensive to install. There's

also the problem of **maintenance**; we'd need to pay a technician to travel to make repairs if anything went wrong and for expensive parts that needed to be replaced. There could be a real decline in the amount of money we save if we ran into operational problems.

Jane: Can I just clarify something here? Abdul, is this **experimental** technology, or have alternative-energy generation systems been successful in other office environments?

Abdul: Well, every small-scale system is different because every building is different. The technology would have to be specially designed for our building in order to be **efficient**.

Allen: I can't help but feel that a solar energy project would be too ambitious. There would probably be technical **limitations** about the sort of system we could install on the office roof. I'm not sure it's even possible, or if the local government would let us.

Jane: I can assure you that the company wouldn't do anything unsafe or illegal.

Zara: It could be good publicity, though. We could market ourselves as a complete "green" business.

Simon: Maybe we should have some of our marketing people look at that. I think ...

Jane: We're getting sidetracked. Can we stick to the main points of the meeting? We should probably move on to the next part of the agenda, so I'd just like to summarize the key points so far. First of all, we want to immediately start making the simple energy-saving changes mentioned, such as cleaning the windows, turning off computer screens, and installing energy-saving lightbulbs. Second, we want to look into possible larger-scale alternative energy systems such as solar panels or a solar water-heating system. However, we need to do a lot of research in that area to see if we could get permission to install a system on the roof. A positive to installing a larger-scale project would be that it could generate good publicity for the company. Have I missed anything?

Abdul: You didn't mention ... 🔊 6.8

A: So, to summarize the key points so far: we agree that we want to reduce energy consumption and we want to consider an alternative energy source. Does anyone have anything to say about a solar energy system?

B: I'm more concerned about our water usage.

C: Sorry, but that's not really what we're discussing right now.

🔊 6.9

See script on page 142.

6.10

Professor: Good morning everyone. Today I'm going to talk about working in groups, both in education and in the workplace. I'll talk about why it's so important nowadays and we'll look at some ways to make sure that groups work successfully.

If you ask an employer, "what is the skill that you most look for in new employees?" they will often say it is the ability to work well with other people. That's because on the job, so much work is done in teams. Employees have to be able to collaborate to listen to other people's opinions, ask questions, respect differences, and resolve conflicts.

But not all working groups function well. There are a number of reasons for this. Sometimes the project is not defined clearly enough, so people don't really know what they have to do. Sometimes people feel that their opinions are not valued. Sometimes people complain that a majority of the work is done by a minority of the people.

OK, so there are several ways that groups can be helped to succeed. One thing is to make sure that the project has a clear timeline and that everyone in the group knows what has to be done by when. This helps keep everyone focused on the same goal.

Another way to help a group succeed is to divide up the work at the beginning of the project and to give everyone in the group a role – a specific job to do. Most groups assign roles according to what people are good at. For example, a person who is good at art might be the natural choice for designing a presentation or a logo.

There are different kinds of roles that people can have. Usually, you have a leader who also chairs the meetings. You should also have a recorder – someone who takes notes on what is discussed and agreed on in the meetings.

But a lot depends on the size of the group and the type of project. When you are planning your project, first work out your timeline. Then identify the different jobs that have to be done and make sure that everyone knows what their role is.

Now, I'd like to talk about …

UNIT 7

▶ Jen Lewin's Light and Sound Installations

Jen Lewin: Technology has been part of art since the beginning of art, whether it was, you know, the advent of charcoal to draw on a cave wall or paints. In this case, we're using, um, computers and computer systems and data and bits and bytes. But it's really, and from my perspective, it's no different than paint.

I come into here, this is a new project, and it's really about combining the old and the new. It's going to be five different giant, um, lights, and they use aluminum frames and old Edison bulbs. And in the bulbs are small LEDs that we can project video into.

Lisa Tamiris Becker: Jen Lewin is an interactive new media artist. She does create computer mediated artworks that involve the viewer. She works with sound and light and encouraging the viewer to move around and activate parts of the artwork.

Jen Lewin: These are interactive platforms that are part of my pool sculpture, and they're meant to be jumped on and played on, and you step on them and they light up and project and send video messages to the other platforms, and you can create beautiful swirls of light and color.

Lisa Tamiris Becker: You know, what is art? What is technology? What is craft? That's an elusive question. I think if you go back to the most ancient roots of art, whether you go back to cave paintings, which existed in many different parts of the world, it was about the image that might have been represented, but it was also about the space and the light in which you were perceiving those images.

Jen Lewin: It's not surprising that this idea of interactive art with large groups of people is happening at a time when there's so much social media. We look at the Internet, suddenly there's all these examples of the Web being used to connect groups of people and to bring them together, and in my work I'm trying to do the same thing. I'm trying to bring 100 people together into a space to play with a sculpture in a much more networked and connected way.

Lisa Tamiris Becker: Art, architecture, and technologies of light, technologies of construction, etc. were combined to create total environments. So I think a lot of new media artists are returning to that idea.

 7.1

Host: Hello from downtown. Overnight, the area's mystery graffiti artist has struck again. Although the **identity** of the painter remains unknown, their work is making an impact on the community. This large image has been painted on the side of an office building. A lot of people in the street on their way to work are stopping to look at it. Let's talk to a few of them and find out what they think of this latest spray-painted image.

Hello, excuse me?

Alex: Yes?

Host: I'm reporting on the recent increase in street art in the downtown area. Can I ask you a few questions?

Alex: Sure, no problem.

Host: What is your name?

Alex: My name is Alex.

Host: So, Alex, what do you think of this new artistic addition to the neighborhood?

Alex: This street art? I think it's great. It's something interesting to look at, and it looks good, doesn't it? I live around the corner, so this is on my doorstep.

Host: What do you like about it?

Alex: I just think it's cool – it has a distinctive style. At first glance, it looks like the painting was done in a few minutes. But in fact, it's not just spray painting; it's the work of a talented artist. It really decorates the area, and I think the **creativity** makes a very ugly neighborhood a lot better looking.

Host: Does everyone in the area like it?

Alex: Most of my neighbors do. We think this kind of thing could become a special feature of the area. It's a real shame that it's going to be covered up before many people have a chance to see it.

Host: Covered up?

Alex: The police are going to paint over it soon because street art is illegal.

Host: Oh, right. Yes, we'll come back to that in a minute. Thanks for talking to us.

Alex: No problem.

Host: Clearly some people really like the painting. However, there's also already been some **criticism** of the piece. Let's see what more we can find out about this side of the story.
Hello, excuse me?

Office worker: Yes?

Host: I'm finding out what people think of street art in this area. Can I ask you a few questions?

Office worker: I'm just on my way into the office, so you'll have to be quick.

Host: What do you think of this painting?

Office worker: I don't really like it. It's just graffiti, isn't it?

Host: What do you mean?

Office worker: The people who own this building didn't ask for this, did they? I mean, what **right** does this person have to spray paint their message here? If somebody wants to express themselves in this way, they should get permission. I'd be really angry if someone did this in my neighborhood.

Host: Do you think it's a work of art?

Office worker: No, not at all. Art is an exhibition in an art museum. This is just somebody spraying paint onto a wall in the middle of the night. Like I said, it's just **self-expression**.

Host: Yes, I see what you mean. Thanks for taking a minute to talk.

Office worker: No problem.

Host: I think it would be a good idea to get a professional view on this now. I have a local police officer with me. Hello, and thanks for talking with me today.

Police officer: Hi, no problem.

Host: What's your view on the latest work of the mystery painter?

Police officer: Well, to be honest, as a piece of art, I actually really like it, despite the fact that it's illegal. However, I also completely agree with the person you just spoke with. We can't have this sort of thing. It *is* vandalism, and it *is* against the law.

Host: It's against the law?

Police officer: Yes. Vandalism is a crime because it is intentionally damaging property that belongs to the city or to other people.

Host: I'm very interested to hear you call this piece of vandalism a work of *art*.

Police officer: It is artistic, though, isn't it? I couldn't paint that. The person who did this, especially very quickly and at night, is very creative. This painting is really expressive, but I have to stress that it's illegal, and therefore we're going to paint over it later today. We **remove** all graffiti because it's the law.

Host: What would you recommend for people who want to express themselves through street art?

Police officer: My recommendation? Well, if this artist wants to paint where everyone can see the artwork, he or she should get permission. We can work with street artists to create art that people have chosen to have in their community.

Host: So you mean you can give someone permission to paint graffiti?

Police officer: Yes, well, sort of. However, they have to apply for a permit and get approval and so on. This makes it a legal activity rather than vandalism.

Host: Thanks a lot for talking with us.

Police officer: My pleasure.

Host: Next, I have an art critic here who agrees with some people about the quality of the latest street painting. This is Simone James, an art gallery owner and art critic. Hello, Simone.

Simone: Hello.

Host: Simone, could you **comment** on the latest creation of our illegal painter?

Simone: Many people think that the painting is just rough spray painting. However, the fact of the matter is the artist has created a very expressive piece of artwork using very basic tools and materials. The color scheme and the **composition** work very well together. It's a strong piece. If this artist were to exhibit and sell their work, I think he or she could make a lot of money.

Host: Do you have any idea who the artist might be?

Simone: I have no idea at all, but technically, the work really is very good, so I'd like to find out!

Host: Thank you very much. Finally, there's one more person I'd like to speak with. This is Joseph, who's 13. Joseph, what do you think of the mystery artist's latest painting?

Joseph: I wish I'd done it! I think it's really good.

Host: What do you like about it?

Joseph: I think this type of art is a really good way of expressing your ideas. I don't know who did it, but I guess it's a young person like me and by doing this kind of art in this way, on the streets, the artist is communicating a message about how young people feel.

Host: OK, thanks Joseph. So we've had a full range of responses to the latest street art in the downtown area. However, the true identity of the graffiti painter remains a mystery.

 7.2

See script on page 153.

🔊 7.3

Robert: ... Okay everyone, are we ready to get back to business? The next item to look at today is the proposed budget to continue paying for public art in City Park. We've recently had to spend a lot of money repairing and restoring the sculpture we commissioned last year because vandals have broken parts of it. We've also spent a lot of time and money removing graffiti from it. The city accounting office has confirmed that the total bill for cleaning and repairs has come to more than $7,000 this year. There's been a proposal that we sell the sculpture, stop paying for new public art, and use the money to pay for a new recreation center. Would anyone like to comment on this?

Lisa: Yes, Robert, I'd like to say something.

Robert: OK, Lisa. Go ahead.

Lisa: Personally, I'm not really sure that paying for art is an appropriate way to spend public money. We assume that we should invest in art since so many other parks have art, but in reality, it's costing us a lot of money, and the art doesn't really benefit the city's population. A lot of people simply don't **appreciate** or like to **interpret** art. The truth of the matter is, more people would use and benefit from a recreation center.

Robert: If I understand you correctly, Lisa, you're saying that we shouldn't spend more money commissioning art?

Lisa: Well, yes. I think public art is a waste of money.

Robert: I see. Yes, Ahmad, would you like to add something?

Ahmad: Yes, thank you Robert. I see what you mean, Lisa, and I'm not an expert, but it's been said that art, and appreciating art, is an important part of any culture. OK, it's true that some people say we're wasting money by commissioning art, but the fact of matter is that art is an important part of any culture. Art can help make us proud of our city, and a lot of people really enjoy looking at it. We had 400,000 visitors to our art museum last year, so people are interested in art.

Marco: That's true, Ahmad. Research has demonstrated over and over again that art can have a very positive effect on people.

Robert: Thank you Ahmad and Marco. Yes, Pei, did you want to add something?

Pei: Ahmad and Marco have good points, but one other thing to remember is that although many people think that art is worth a lot of money because it's by famous artists or because the city invested in it, we don't actually know that the art is worth anything. Look at the sculpture there now, for example. Since it's been damaged and repaired so much, we don't know if we can sell the sculpture, even to a private collector. Do we really want to invest in more art?

Robert: OK, thank you all for your comments. I think we need to find out how much new art would cost us. We'll have to get an art expert to **analyze** the pieces we like and maybe we can **restore** them rather than buy new ones.

Would anyone else like to make a comment?

Yes, Marco?

Marco: If we decide against commissioning the public art, we'll need to put something in its place.

Lisa: Like building the recreation center instead.

Pei: You say that, Lisa, but I am not sure that would be popular enough. We'd need to talk to a lot of people to gather data and opinions about whether they like the art or if they want a new building, but this might **reveal** some really good ideas we haven't thought of.

Robert: Yes, I think you're right, Pei. Let's put together a survey. This will include commissioning more art and building the recreation center. Also, we can include three or four other ideas. Then we can get people to look at it. Is there anything else anyone would like to say? Yes, Claudia?

Claudia: For me, there's a public safety issue here. The police reports have shown that kids climb on the public art we have there now. This happens almost every night, and they're breaking it and writing graffiti on it. This artwork really is causing more problems than it's worth.

Ahmad: You may be right, Claudia, but I wonder if it's the location of the artwork rather than the artwork itself that's the problem.

Lisa: In other words, Ahmad, you think we should move it?

Ahmad: I think moving it might solve the vandalism problem. It seems as if the art is just costing us money for cleaning and repairs. If we were to **display** it in a different spot, we probably wouldn't have these problems. Plus, we'd still contribute to the culture of the city by having the art available.

Pei: I agree with Ahmad. I think we could consider moving the sculpture to the front of city hall, next to the hospital, or possibly even inside the main shopping mall. In fact, the shopping mall has already expressed interest in this because they believe artwork could be a tourist attraction. If we planned it properly, we could get people to see the artwork and do some shopping at the same time!

Lisa: So, Pei, what you're saying is that you'd definitely rather keep commissioning art but just put it in other locations?

Pei: Yes, that's right.

Robert: OK, yes, those ideas make sense. I think we need to do more research here. First, we need to **focus on** identifying some places that the art could be displayed. We need to **reject** any places where we feel vandals would be likely to damage it. Second, we need to consider the cost of the current art, the sculpture that is already there.

Pei: There's one other point I'd like to raise.

Robert: OK. Go ahead, Pei.

Pei: What would we do with the money if we didn't commission any new art and didn't build the recreation center?

Robert: You ask a good question. The money would be put back into the budget, and we'd have to determine a project that reflects what people really want.

Ahmad: Well, a recreation center or any other center is a good thing, but it isn't art. I think our children need to see art in public places, especially the work of a famous artist, right here in our city. We need to have a balance of investment in leisure activities and public art in the lives of our children.

Robert: OK, I think we need to look into this. We need to explore our options in more detail.

Are there any other comments on this topic? No? OK. We'll move on, then …

 7.4

See script on page 164.

 7.5

Anchor: Good morning! In today's program, we're looking at an important decision for every undergraduate, and that's how to choose your major. Here to give us some advice is Anita Rao, a career advisor from City University. Welcome to the show.

Anita Rao: Thank you.

Anchor: First of all, I'd like to ask: what advice do you give to students who really can't decide on a major?

Anita Rao: I think the most important thing is to choose something you like. Identify the subjects that you are most interested in and the classes that you have enjoyed most.

Anchor: That seems logical.

Anita Rao: Yes. But many students forget that. A lot of students nowadays are so concerned about employment prospects after they graduate!

Anchor: Isn't it a good idea to think about making money?

Anita Rao: I think it's certainly good to think about how you might make a living. But you have to be realistic. A lot of students say, "I want to study computer science because I'll make a lot of money." But do you have the math skills? Computer science involves a lot of math ability. It can be difficult and frustrating. Yes, there are many good jobs out there, but not everybody has the ability to be a computer programmer.

Anchor: Is it a good idea to get some experience in the field?

Anita Rao: Absolutely. I encourage students to look for summer jobs or internships. That way they get a sense of what the working world is really like. Often they come back in the fall with a much more realistic idea of what they would like to do.

Anchor: What other advice do you have for students?

Anita Rao: Don't worry too much. Unless you are studying in a professional area, such as medicine, your major will not usually limit you to a specific career.

Anchor: Really?

Anita Rao: Yes. Many people don't find work in their major field, and most people change careers several times. What is important to employers are the general skills that you get in college: the ability to speak and write clearly, to research information, and to work with other people.

UNIT 8

▶ Baby Boomers' Retirement Style

Ben Tracy (reporter): This is retirement, boomer style.

Gordon Feld: This is what retirement should be.

Ben Tracy: Gordon Feld and his equally adventurous wife Peggy spend their days zipping through the Arizona desert.

So this is retirement? Where is the shuffleboard?

Gordon Feld: Nah, that's for old people.

Ben Tracy: They bought a home in this retirement community 45 miles from Phoenix. Developments like this cater to boomers concerned about cost and lifestyle. The average house sells for about $200,000, and $100 a month buys the amenities many boomers demand.

Woman: They're highly educated, they have high expectations, um, of what they want in their life, and they expect to live a long time.

Man 1: Helmets on.

Ben Tracy: In fact, 86% of boomers say they'll be more active in retirement than their parents were. But to pay for it, 70% will keep working at least part time, and 42% are delaying full-time retirement because of hits to their retirement accounts and home values during the recession.

Man 2: They're having to work longer trying to rebuild their investment portfolio and their 401(k)s.

Ben Tracy: 62-year-old Jerry Axton is still running his handmade furniture business, even though he's been living in this retirement village for two years.

Jerry Axton: Doing nothing doesn't sound very exciting, and retirement borderlines to me doing nothing.

Ben Tracy: Most of these boomers feel their sunset years are still a ways down the road. Ben Tracy, CBS News, Buckeye, Arizona.

🔊 8.1

Host: Hello and welcome to the *Money and Finance* podcast. I'm your host, Ian Brown, and today's topic is **retirement**. In the past, giving up work in their sixties signaled the end of an active, exciting life for people. It was seen as a time for staying at home, doing the gardening, and being very careful with money. Twenty years ago, most people planned to leave a large sum of money to their children upon their death and didn't spend a lot on themselves once they started to rely on their retirement funds, whether those came from an employee **pension** plan or Social Security.

But times have changed. People nowadays don't think of the sixties as old. People who have exercised and eaten a good diet throughout their lives have plenty of energy to enjoy life, no matter what age they retire at. Many of today's older people see retirement as a reward for a lifetime of hard work, and rather than saving their money to give to their children, they're spending it – on luxuries, travel, new cars, and meals out, and because they worked hard and saved hard for their retirement, they have plenty of money to spend. As a group, the over-60s in the United States have over 25 trillion dollars in **assets**: **property**, money in the bank, investments, and so on. Retirement assets accounted for 36% of the household financial assets in the United States. The average married person between the ages of 65 and 74 spent 26% of the household income on food and entertainment.

Rick and Nadia Jones are typical of this new approach to retirement. I asked them to share their thoughts.

Nadia: Well, in my working life I was a banker and Rick was in business. We both retired at 65, and since that time, we've traveled a lot and have had years of excitement and fun. A lot of our friends are doing the same. We're still healthy and we love traveling, so why shouldn't we? I had to persuade Rick to agree to the idea at first. It just wasn't like that for our parents. However, we've managed to save enough money to **permit** us to live the life we've always wanted, and I think we've earned it.

Rick: We've been to Alaska and Europe – and Nadia loves the weather in the Caribbean! We've been there three times.

Host: According to one survey, 20 years ago, most of today's older people believed they would work in the garden, read, and babysit their grandchildren. However, retired people now want to do more exciting things! Do you agree with this?

Nadia: I do, I think. We worked hard during our careers to **ensure** that our two daughters had a good education. They're both married and working now. I want to be involved in my children's lives, but I do also want adventure! We live close to both our daughters and offer to babysit our grandchildren regularly, but we're not a free day care!

Rick: Exactly. We don't have any **dependents** anymore. Our daughters need to work hard and save their money just as we've done. Our savings allow us to live the life we've always wanted. This is our chance to have some fun, and we don't want to stay home all day gardening and watching television. Our daughters have agreed to support our choices, and we hope they'll make the same choices for themselves one day.

Nadia: I think our parents' **generation** thought it was really important to save for the next generation, to give money to their children, but our generation doesn't think that way.

Rick: We've talked to our daughters about it. They understand that the money is ours to spend. They also understand that as long as we're in shape and healthy, we might as well enjoy life. Our home is also worth about $272,000. We are not planning on selling it, so they'll get that eventually.

Host: Recent research shows that about two-thirds of older people agree with Rick and Nadia and plan to leave their home to their children, and no money. But what about the next generation? Today's working generation is probably facing a more difficult retirement than their parents. Pensions are getting smaller, many companies are no longer providing pensions at all, and the average age of retirement is increasing. According to the U.S. Census Bureau, about 16% of Americans aged 65 and over are still working, but that number is increasing. Should these parents be doing more? Rick?

Rick: I think we both feel we've done our part as parents. We have many happy, healthy years ahead of us and still have other things we want to do with our lives, and now we're doing them. I'd advise everyone else to do the same.

🔊 8.2

See script on page 175.

🔊 8.3

Mika: Hello. My name is Mika. I'm going to discuss how things are changing for elderly people in Japan. I'll begin by explaining the importance of family in Japan and present some figures that explain how the population is changing. Finally, I'll talk about the way the Japanese government is dealing with the aging population.

Family in Japan has been very important since the days of my **ancestors**. However, while the extended family is very important in other countries, the focus in Japan is on the bond among children, parents, grandparents, and so on. Of course, this means that in many cases, when elderly people can no longer take care of themselves, they move in with their children.

Japan has one of the highest life expectancies in the world. Its population is about 127 million. If you look at the data I've provided, you will note that it **indicates** there were about 33 million people in 2014 over the age of 65 in Japan, nearly 26% of the population. By 2050, Japan's population will be about 99 million, and 35% of the population will be over 65. The population of children under the age of 14 is expected to fall from about 19 million to about 18 million in 2020 and 12 million by 2050. This can be traced back to a low fertility rate, that is, the number of children being born to a woman during the time she is able to have children. That fertility rate has dropped to just below 1.5

children per woman. Young Japanese people are waiting longer than their parents' generation to get married, and when they do, they're having fewer children. Young people now enjoy a lot of free time in their twenties and thirties, but this also results in the same issues that other countries are facing: more and more elderly people to take care of, with fewer younger people to be **providers**. Since the population of Japan is set to decrease by 22% by 2050, this means a loss of about 28 million residents.

The Japanese government has taken steps to deal with the situation. Most Japanese people between the ages of 40 and 65 pay an income tax that goes to help those over 65. The over-65s don't get the money directly, but the government supports them. Even elderly people living at home with family have a care worker who makes sure they have everything they need. Some elderly people go to a day-care center a few times a week, where they can share meals and **participate** in social activities. Those elderly people who don't live with family generally live in **institutions**, with about nine people living in one home. Each has a bedroom, and they share a living room and kitchen. This enables them to have some independence and to feel cared for at the same time.

Ahmet: My name is Ahmet. Thank you Mika for your interesting presentation. My topic today is how elderly people are cared for in Turkey. First, I'll give some background on how the elderly are usually cared for. After that, I'll talk about some of the drawbacks and benefits of this system, and I'll finish by explaining the challenges ahead.

Mika explained that it is becoming more and more common in Japan for elderly people to live in institutions when their ability to care for themselves declines. Moving old people into nursing homes allows the younger generation to continue their lives without having to worry about daily care for an aging parent. However, in Turkey, 80% of households have an older person in them. Many families see this as the natural solution to dealing with old age. As parents, we **devote** ourselves to our children. In turn, as adults, we devote ourselves to our aging parents. Most people my age have a grandparent living at home.

The system has drawbacks, both for the families caring for elderly people and for the elderly people themselves. Those responsible for the welfare of an elderly person can feel that they aren't free to do as they like in their own home. The older people being cared for may also not feel completely free and dislike the way things are done by their caregivers. Living closely together in forced circumstances can raise tensions. However, there are many benefits to these arrangements. In many households, older people **contribute** to the family by participating in domestic jobs and helping with childcare. This gives them something to do and a sense of **responsibility**.

Turkey's population is just over 80 million today. If you look at the graph I've provided, you will see that more than 5 million people, or around 6%, are over 65. For now, the solution is for Turks to continue caring for the elderly at home.

 8.4

See script on page 186.

 8.5

Presenter: Welcome to the College Career Center! Here you will find resources for everything to do with finding a job or planning a career. We encourage you to visit us early and often, and to keep your long-term goals in mind as you progress through college.

Most students come to us first for information about jobs. We have job listings for part-time jobs on and off campus, which can be a good way to make some extra cash on the weekends. We can also help you find internships. Some internships are unpaid, but an internship with a good company can be a great experience and lead to a paid position later.

We offer workshops to help you prepare your résumé so that it shows you in your best light. As a student, you may not have a lot of work experience, but if you have done some community service or held a leadership position, that all goes into your résumé. Also, don't forget your online identity! Many employers look at your profile on social media before they decide to call you for an interview. We can help you create a good online identity.

Every spring, the career center organizes job fairs, when companies come to campus to meet with students. This is a good way to network with companies that you are interested in. You can also ask questions about the company and find out about future opportunities.

Maybe you'd like to go to graduate or professional school. Here you can research the different programs that are available and find out about financial aid for further study.

So, there are a lot of great resources here at the career center. My name is Scott, and I'd be happy to answer any questions that you have.

UNIT 1 LISTENING QUIZ

Name: _____ Date: _____

PART A KEY SKILLS
ACTIVATING PRIOR KNOWLEDGE

1 Look at the pie charts and circle the correct answers.

Top U.S. Movies 2016:
Domestic Sales (in millions)

a *Finding Dory*
b *Captain America: Civil War*
c *The Secret Life of Pets*
d *The Jungle Book*
e *Deadpool*

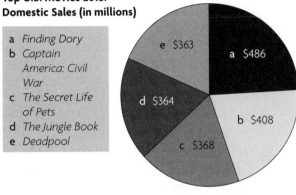

Top U.S. Movies 2016:
Overseas Sales (in millions)

a *Captain America: Civil War*
b *The Jungle Book*
c *Finding Dory*
d *The Secret Life of Pets*
e *Deadpool*

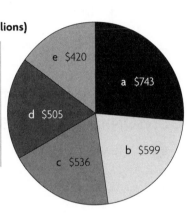

1 What do you think the main topic of this discussion is going to be?
   a Domestic box office sales of U.S. movies in 2016
   b The effects of globalization on the U.S. film industry
   c International box office sales of U.S. movies in 2016
2 What was the most popular movie in the U.S. in 2016?
   a *Captain America: Civil War*
   b *The Jungle Book*
   c *Finding Dory*
3 Which of the following two movies sold the most overseas?
   a *Captain America: Civil War* and *Finding Dory*
   b *The Jungle Book* and *Captain America: Civil War*
   c *The Secret Life of Pets* and *Captain America: Civil War*
4 Which of the following movies sold the least overseas?
   a *Deadpool*
   b *The Secret Life of Pets*
   c *Finding Dory*
5 Which statement is true?
   a Two of the top three movies made more in domestic sales than in overseas sales.
   b Domestic sales for three of the movies were higher than their overseas sales.
   c All of the movies on both charts earned more overseas than they did domestically.

PART B ADDITIONAL SKILLS

2 ▶ 1.1 Listen to a class discussion with a guest speaker. Write *T* (true) or *F* (false) next to the statements. Correct the false statements.

_____ 1 The professor has talked about other aspects of globalization in previous classes.

_____

_____ 2 Domestic sales of American films have skyrocketed in recent years.

_____

_____ 3 China is the third-largest market for American films.

_____

_____ 4 China has no limits on the number of foreign films that can be imported every year.

_____

_____ 5 Some Hollywood film studios co-produce movies in China.

_____

PART C PRONUNCIATION FOR LISTENING
CONSONANT CLUSTERS

3 ▶ 1.2 Listen to the sentences and fill in the blanks.

1 How does _____ travel _____ to climate change?
2 Hollywood _____ the ten most _____ movies last year.
3 It's difficult to _____ the amount of _____ they have on the industry.
4 Edmonton is the _____ largest city in Canada by population.
5 One of Hollywood's _____ is producing successful blockbusters _____ .

Name: _____   Date: _____

PART A KEY VOCABULARY

1 Complete the sentences with the correct form of the words in the box.

agriculture   consumer   domestic   import   overseas   process   source   transportation

1 Although Ashton Air is an American company, it sells more airplanes _____ than it does in the United States.
2 The automation of farming equipment has profoundly changed _____ in many parts of the world.
3 The Colorado River is the _____ of most of the drinking water in the west.
4 Some people argue that, to protect our _____ markets, we need to keep jobs in the country and not export them.
5 Most forms of _____ , such as planes and cars, pollute our environment.
6 I am concerned, as a _____ of local produce, about the presence of chemicals in the soil.
7 In recent years many companies have begun _____ raw materials from other countries.
8 The makers of these snacks claim that all of the ingredients are fresh and that none have been _____ .

2 Complete the sentences with the correct form of the words in the box.

export   greenhouse   household   investigate   produce   purchase

1 We _____ all of the wool for our clothes on our farm.
2 The _____ permits farmers to grow vegetables during the coldest months of the year.
3 The government is _____ whether the products contain dangerous chemicals.
4 In another year we will have raised enough money to _____ a new computer system for our business.
5 Almost 85% of the grain that is grown in our state is _____ to other countries.
6 Many _____ in the United States own at least two televisions.

PART B LANGUAGE DEVELOPMENT
MODALS OF PRESENT AND PAST PROBABILITY

3 Choose the best words to complete the sentences. Use the information in parentheses to help you.

1 This pineapple *can't have been grown / might not have been grown* here. It's too cold. (impossible)
2 The package *must have arrived / couldn't have arrived* yet. We only mailed it this morning. (the only logical conclusion)
3 They *could have bought / can't have bought* the apples at our neighbor's farm. (guessing)
4 These coconuts *must be imported / might be imported*. (the only logical conclusion)
5 Your cell phone *might have been made / can't have been made* in Japan, but I'm not positive. (guessing)

GLOBALIZATION AND ENVIRONMENT VOCABULARY

4 Complete the announcement with the correct form of the words in the box.

carbon footprint	carbon emissions	climate change	processing	supply chain

Grassy Farm to Go Green!

Here at Grassy Farm, we believe that (1)_____ is a threat to the whole planet. Our goal is to have the smallest possible (2)_____ within three years. Therefore, we plan to reduce our (3)_____ by 40% a year. We will limit the (4)_____ of the meat we sell to a few items, such as chicken. Moreover, we plan to restrict the companies in our (5)_____ to local companies within a 50-mile radius of our farm. We hope you will support us in our efforts.

UNIT 2 LISTENING QUIZ

Name: _____   Date: _____

PART A KEY SKILLS
LISTENING FOR ADVICE AND SUGGESTIONS

1 ▶ 2.1 Listen to a conversation between two high school students about MOOCs (Massive Open Online Courses). What advice does Anna give Jake? Circle the correct answers.

   1 Jake would like to go to college, but he thinks it's too expensive.
     a "Have you thought about vocational school?"
     b "Have you thought about a MOOC?"
     c "Have you thought about studying computer science?"
   2 Jake wants to know if he can take engineering or computer science classes.
     a "You should google MOOCs."
     b "You should contact MIT."
     c "You should talk to a professor. "
   3 Jake would like to take a course from Harvard University.
     a "You ought to study from home."
     b "You ought to visit their website."
     c "You ought to find a professor you like."

MAKING INFERENCES

2 ▶ 2.1 Listen again. Check the statements that you can infer from the conversation.

   1 Jake's parents are poor. ☐
   2 Jake doesn't know much about MOOCs. ☐
   3 Professors who teach MOOCs do not get paid. ☐
   4 Anna thinks courses in a physical classroom are better than online courses. ☐
   5 Jake is interested in studying technology in college. ☐

PART B ADDITIONAL SKILLS

3 ▶ 2.1 Listen again. Circle the correct answers.

   1 MOOCs are online courses run by *students / universities*.
   2 MOOCs are usually *free / expensive*.
   3 According to Anna, *professors / students* grade assignments from MOOCs.
   4 *All / Some* of the top American colleges offer MOOCs.
   5 At the end of the conversation Jake seems *positive / negative* about MOOCs.

PART C PRONUNCIATION FOR LISTENING
CERTAIN AND UNCERTAIN INTONATION

4 ▶ 2.2 Listen to the excerpts from the conversation. Does the speaker sound certain or uncertain? Write *C* (certain) or *U* (uncertain).

   1 I guess I could start by taking a class or two. _____
   2 No, that's the great thing: MOOCs are usually free. _____
   3 But there must be some costs, right? _____
   4 The university tells you how to do it. I think it works pretty well. _____
   5 I don't know. It sounds pretty complex to me. _____

UNIT 2 LANGUAGE QUIZ

Name: _____ Date: _____

PART A KEY VOCABULARY

1 Complete the text with the correct form of the words in the box.

academic   complex   manual   mechanical   practical   specialist   understanding   vocational

Some people, like my brother Adam, are really talented. He's always been good at fixing (1)_____ things, like cars or washing machines. He just seems to have a natural (2)_____ of how machines work – even really (3)_____ ones, like computers. I wish I had a(n) (4)_____ skill like being able to fix things, but I've never been good at (5)_____ tasks. I'm the (6)_____ one in the family – always reading. Adam's going to a(n) (7)_____ school in the fall. When he graduates he'll be a(n) (8)_____ in computer networking. I wish I knew what I wanted to do!

2 Complete the sentences with the correct form of the words in the box.

acquire   advisor   internship   medical   physical   professional   secure   technical

1 Rafa has always wanted to be a surgeon, so it was no surprise when he applied to _____ school.
2 The school encourages every business student to do a summer _____ at a corporation before their final year of school.
3 Many of the _____ jobs in the healthcare industry, such as pharmacists or nurses, pay very well.
4 It can often take years to _____ real fluency in another language.
5 I need a(n) _____ who can tell me what courses I need to take to get into nursing school.
6 Studying for hours has a(n) _____ cost: I feel exhausted, and all my muscles ache.
7 I want to get a degree in a field that is _____ , not one that is changing rapidly.
8 Some of these computer manuals are too _____ for me. I need things explained in simpler terms.

PART B LANGUAGE DEVELOPMENT
STATING PREFERENCES WITH *WOULD*

3 Circle the correct form of the verb to complete each sentence.

1 What would you *to prefer / prefer to* study, chemistry or engineering?
2 Would you rather *live / living* at home or at school?
3 Leon prefers *study / studying* in the library where it's quiet.
4 I'd really like *to travel / traveling* for a month after I graduate.
5 Would you rather *work / working* for a large company or a small one?

Prism 3 Listening and Speaking © Cambridge University Press 2017 **Photocopiable**

Name: _____ Date: _____

PART A KEY SKILLS
IDENTIFYING CONTRASTING OPINIONS

1 ▶ 3.1 Listen to a discussion about homeopathy, an alternative system of medicine. Who expresses each opinion? Write *DC* (Dr. Cooper) or *DM* (Dr. Martinez).

　1 It's a powerful principle, don't you think? _____
　2 A placebo is a false medicine that does nothing. _____
　3 As I see it, millions of people around the world benefit from homeopathy. _____
　4 I believe that most scientists do understand homeopathy. _____
　5 Homeopaths make extraordinary claims about their placebo medicines because it's a good way of making money. _____

STRENGTHENING POINTS IN AN ARGUMENT

2 ▶ 3.1 Listen again. How do the speakers strengthen their points in the argument? Match the statements with the techniques.

　1 Oh, yes, you're right. It was 1796. _____
　2 The body senses the onion in the medicine but the amount is so small, and the body's defense reaction so strong, that the overall effect is to help the person recover from their illness. _____
　3 One popular homeopathic medicine, for example, is made from pure water! _____
　4 In my practice, I've personally seen hundreds of people who have benefited from homeopathic remedies. _____
　5 I believe that most scientists do understand homeopathy, as I've just explained. _____

　a using logic
　b giving a personal example
　c offering additional information
　d repeating the other person's point and saying it is correct
　e returning to an earlier reference

PART B PRONUNCIATION FOR LISTENING
INTONATION IN TAG QUESTIONS

3 ▶ 3.2 Listen to the excerpts from the discussion. Is the speaker expressing uncertainty or agreement? Write *U* (uncertainty) or *A* (agreement).

　1 Excuse me, but I believe homeopathy began in 1796, not 1696, didn't it? _____
　2 It's a powerful principle, don't you think? _____
　3 Well, to me her homeopathic treatment sounds pretty simple, doesn't it? _____
　4 Dr. Cooper mentioned that homeopathic medicines contain tiny amounts of active substances, but she didn't say just how tiny, did she? _____
　5 Just because scientists don't yet understand exactly how homeopathy works doesn't prove that it's wrong, does it? _____
　6 This is a multi-million dollar industry after all, isn't it? _____

Name: _____   Date: _____

PART A KEY VOCABULARY

1 Complete the text with the correct form of the words in the box.

| clinical   contract   data   infected   occur   outbreak   precaution   recover   treatment   trials |

International Traveler Alert

Public health officials have reported that a(n) (1)_____ of the Zika virus has
(2)_____ in the Bahamas. As of July 14, 23 people have (3)_____ the virus.
Because the virus is primarily spread by mosquitos, the Centers for Disease Control and
Prevention (CDC) recommends that everyone traveling to the area do the following:
Take (4)_____ to avoid mosquito bites, like wearing long-sleeved shirts and pants.
If you have flu-like symptoms, get (5)_____ from a doctor or a local hospital.
According to the most recent (6)_____ , the majority of people who have been
(7)_____ with the Zika virus have (8)_____ within three weeks.
The CDC reports that a vaccine against the Zika virus is currently being tested in
(9)_____ (10)_____ and will hopefully be ready for general use soon.

2 Complete the text with the correct form of the words in the box.

| controlled   factor   prevention   prove   researcher   scientific |

My cousin Zack works as a (1)_____ at the Zillow Laboratory. He's always
been interested in (2)_____ things, like chemistry. The employees at Zillow
look at a lot of (3)_____ that affect health, such as diet and exercise. They do
(4)_____ experiments in which, for instance, one group eats a high-fat diet and
the other group eats a low-fat diet. I think they're trying to (5)_____ that fat is not
good for you. They think that certain kinds of (6)_____ – like avoiding a lot of salt
and fat – are extremely important to a person's well-being.

          Prism 3 Listening and Speaking © Cambridge University Press 2017 **Photocopiable**

PART B LANGUAGE DEVELOPMENT
HEALTH SCIENCE VOCABULARY

3 Match the sentence halves.

1 Doctors often give patients _____
2 Pharmaceutical companies must conduct _____
3 Some athletes do not want to travel to tropical areas _____
4 It took him months _____
5 The best way to **treat** a cold is _____

a because of the Zika **virus**.
b to **recover** from his skiing accident.
c to rest and drink plenty of fluids.
d **antibiotics** to cure infections.
e clinical **trials** before they can release a new drug.

CONDITIONALS

4 Find and correct the mistakes in the past unreal conditionals.

1 If the polio vaccine had existed in the 1940s, my grandmother would not get the disease.
_____

2 If we had taken our malaria pills, we wouldn't become so sick.
_____

3 Noah's infection could be cured if we had had the proper antibiotics.
_____

4 If people practice preventative medicine, they could have avoided many illnesses.
_____

5 If everyone got the flu vaccine, there would have been fewer outbreaks this year.
_____

Name: _____   Date: _____

PART A KEY SKILLS
DISTINGUISHING MAIN IDEAS FROM DETAILS

1 ▶ 4.1 Listen to a talk about the Great Pacific Garbage Patch (GPGP). Match the main ideas (a–e) with the parts of the talk (1–3) in which they appear.

Part of the talk	Main ideas
1 Giving background information	
2 Explaining a problem	
3 Offering a solution	

a The discovery of the GPGP
b How to clean up the GPGP
c The size of the GPGP
d How the GPGP was created
e The effect of plastic on marine animals

2 ▶ 4.1 Listen again. Then match the details below with the main ideas (a–e) in Exercise 1.

1 Moore decided to take a shortcut to get home. _____
2 The California Current carries a plastic water bottle from Los Angeles to Mexico. _____
3 The birds think bits of plastic are fish eggs. _____
4 From outer space, the GPGP looks like the Great Wall of China. _____
5 The platforms could be made of wood or metal. _____

PART B PRONUNCIATION FOR LISTENING
SENTENCE STRESS

3 ▶ 4.2 Listen to the excerpts from the talk. Underline the words the speaker stresses.

1 What he found in this wild, lonely area was trash: miles and miles of plastic waste.
2 No matter what time of day I looked, plastic debris was floating everywhere.
3 Do the actions of one person really impact the world?
4 Now, the problem with plastic is that it does not biodegrade.
5 The plastic waste is breaking down into tiny pieces, full of toxic chemicals, that marine animals are eating.
6 There really is no way for these animals to adapt to changes like these in their environment.

Name: _____ Date: _____

PART A KEY VOCABULARY

1 Complete the text with the correct form of the words in the box.

adapt   coastal   conservation   exploit   habitat   impact   modify   waste   wilderness

Help us protect our natural resources!

Our goal at Lakeside Villages is the (1)_____ of marine (2)_____ in Lake Congee. We are fortunate to have more than 500 miles of (3)_____ property here and we want to make sure that we control the (4)_____ that we have on our natural environment. Our goal is to (5)_____ to our environment, not to change it.

Accordingly, we have (6)_____ our regulations to include the following:

- All plastic, glass, paper, and metal (7)_____ must be recycled.
- No fishing is allowed. We cannot (8)_____ our natural reserves of marine wildlife by fishing.
- There will be no development of (9)_____ along the north shore of the lake. We want to keep this area in its natural state.

Thank you for your cooperation.

2 Match the words in bold with their definitions.

1 **Copper** has been used in electrical wiring since the invention of the telegraph in the 1800s.
2 Animals, like humans, need vitamins and **minerals** to survive. _____
3 The **diamond** in this ring was created in a laboratory. _____
4 Burning **natural gas** produces fewer toxins than burning other types of fossil fuels. _____
5 Many birds fly south to avoid the **harsh** conditions of winter. _____
6 Underground **mining** can damage the environment. _____

a natural substances found in the earth such as coal or gold
b fuel for heating or cooking that is found underground
c severe and unpleasant
d the industry or activity of removing valuable substances from the earth
e a very hard, valuable stone, often used in jewelry
f a reddish-brown metal, used in electrical equipment and for making wires and coins

PART B LANGUAGE DEVELOPMENT
MULTI-WORD PREPOSITIONS

3 Complete the paragraph with the correct prepositions.

According [1]_____ a recent report, the populations of around 75% of animal species in this country are declining due [2]_____ human activities. Apart [3]_____ obvious causes such as hunting, the main reasons for the decline appear to be habitat destruction, together [4]_____ pollution. This problem affects all parts of the country, except [5]_____ the mountains in the far north, where few animals or people live.

THE PAST PERFECT

4 Complete the text with the past perfect form of the verbs in parentheses.

About 20 years ago – in early 1997 – a man named Charles Moore was sailing home across the North Pacific Ocean. He [1]_____ (finish) a sailing race and was heading back from Hawaii to Santa Barbara, California. Rather than taking the usual route, he [2]_____ (decide) to take a thousand-mile "shortcut" through a high-pressure area in the central Pacific Ocean, where few people [3]_____ (go).
What he found in this wild, lonely area was trash: miles and miles of plastic waste. As he reported, "In the week it took to cross the subtropical high, no matter what time of day I looked, plastic debris was floating everywhere: bottles, bottle caps, wrappers ... parts of TVs, volleyballs, truck tires." Based on what he [4]_____ (find), he calculated the total weight of the trash to be about three million tons.
The area Moore [5]_____ (discover) is now called the Great Pacific Garbage Patch, or GPGP.

VERBS TO DESCRIBE ENVIRONMENTAL CHANGE

5 Complete the summary with the correct form of the verbs in the box.

adapt   affect   decline   exploit   survive

We are only beginning to comprehend how our actions [1]_____ the world. We know that the populations of certain animals, such as polar bears, have [2]_____ in recent years. We believe that these bears cannot [3]_____ to a warmer climate. Other animals, such as the Javan rhinoceros, have been [4]_____ by hunters for huge profits. Today only 40–60 Javan rhinoceros still [5]_____ on the island of Java.

Prism 3 Listening and Speaking © Cambridge University Press 2017 **Photocopiable**

UNIT 5 LISTENING QUIZ

Name: _____ Date: _____

PART A GENERAL SKILLS

1 ▶ 5.1 Listen to a talk about green architecture in Costa Rica. Match the potential problems to the proposed solutions.

Potential problems

1 Very hot climate _____
2 It's dark inside of the house _____
3 The house is too small _____
4 High energy costs _____
5 The need for storage space _____

Proposed solutions

a solar panels
b loft space
c extended roof
d wrap-around porch
e glass walls

PART B KEY SKILLS
UNDERSTANDING FIGURATIVE LANGUAGE

2 ▶ 5.1 Listen again. Circle the phrases you hear.

1 Some people call Costa Rica *Paradise on Earth / cold as ice*.
2 This will shade the porch like *a big tree / a huge umbrella* during the hottest part of the day.
3 Sitting on this porch will be like sitting *in a bird's nest / in a tree house*.
4 They cost *as much as a Tesla / as much as a house*.
5 Sleeping in one of these lofts would be like sleeping *on a cloud / on the ocean*.

UNDERSTANDING STRONG AND TENTATIVE SUGGESTIONS

3 ▶ 5.2 Listen to the excerpts from the discussion. Are the speakers making strong or tentative suggestions? Write *S* (strong) or *T* (tentative).

1 As you can see, the house will definitely have a contemporary look, with its glass walls and natural colors. _____
2 Excuse me, but isn't it really hot in that part of the country? _____
3 And it's going to make the inside of the home significantly cooler. _____
4 They will greatly expand the existing living space of the house. _____
5 I think that in the next few years we're going to see some dramatic changes. _____

PART C PRONUNCIATION FOR LISTENING
EMPHASIS IN CONTRASTING OPINIONS

4 ▶ 5.3 Listen to the sentences. Underline the words in each opinion that the speaker stresses.

1 A: I'm sorry, but won't that make the house pretty dark inside?
   B: Actually, we anticipate that the inside will receive adequate sunlight during the day to do most things.
2 A: Yes, but solar panels are really expensive. I mean, only rich people can really afford them.
   B: But we believe that solar is a great investment in a home .... I think solar power will become more common everywhere.

Name: _____ Date: _____

PART A KEY VOCABULARY

1 Circle the correct word in parentheses to complete each sentence.

Many people are (1)*concerned / sympathetic* about the plans for a new housing development in our community. We all agree that the (2)*contemporary / existing* housing here is not (3)*adequate / existing* for the future. We (4)*anticipate / transform* that our population will increase 30% in the next ten years. Therefore, we need to create (5)*controversial / appropriate* housing for this expanded population. Some of the most (6)*concerned / ambitious* plans call for the construction of four large buildings on the east side of town. Those in favor of this plan believe it is an excellent (7)*feature / investment* in the future. The proposed buildings will have the (8)*investment / potential* to house nearly 1,200 people.

2 Complete the sentences with the correct form of the words in the box.

collapse	contemporary	controversial	feature	obtain	sympathetic	transform

1 It has taken the volunteers almost two years to _____ the funds they need to rebuild the theater.
2 The new performance center has _____ the city's downtown area into a popular cultural neighborhood.
3 The heavy snowfall caused the roofs of many buildings to _____ .
4 Energy-saving _____ , such as new windows and solar panels, add to the resale value of a house.
5 The construction workers are very _____ to the needs of our neighborhood, so they never work late at night.
6 I like traditional houses, but my husband prefers _____ ones.
7 Many buildings and structures that are now loved were very _____ when they were first built. For example, a lot of people hated the Eiffel Tower when it was first built.

PART B LANGUAGE DEVELOPMENT
FUTURE FORMS

3 Complete the sentences by inserting the adverbs in parentheses in the correct places.

1 We're going to see a game in the new stadium this summer. (definitely)

2 They're going to replace the old windows with new ones this fall. (probably)

3 My parents will move to a smaller house someday. (maybe)

4 I won't live in an apartment without air conditioning. (certainly)

5 We'll have enough money one day to build a new garage. (perhaps)

ACADEMIC VOCABULARY FOR ARCHITECTURE AND TRANSFORMATION

4 Complete the article with the correct form of the words in the box.

abandon   anticipate   convert   expand   maintain   transform

Central America's Most Amazing Young Architects

Young architects throughout Central America are designing exciting new spaces. Here are some of our favorites.

Mexico: Spa San Angel

The Mexico City-based firm of Jorge Ambrosi and Gabriela Etchegaray has (1)_____ a set of buildings that people had (2)_____ and were empty into a sleek, new, popular resort.

Costa Rica: Containers of Hope

In San Jose, Costa Rica, architect Benjamin Garcia Saxe has (3)_____ shipping containers into an elegant, inexpensive housing alternative called "Containers of Hope." Garcia Saxe (4)_____ that each unit will cost just $40,000 – significantly less than most social housing in the country.

Guatemala: Casa Corallo

In the mountains of Guatemala City, architect Alejandro Paz is designing houses that (5)_____ the order of their natural environment. His homes in the mountains of Guatemala City follow the shape of the existing trees.

El Salvador: La Piscucha

La Piscucha, a home in San Salvador, was designed by the architectural firm Cinco Patas al Gato. The heart of the three-story home is an entertainment center. The rooms on all three floors (6)_____ out from this center like a flower.

Name: _____ Date: _____

PART A KEY SKILLS
UNDERSTANDING DIGRESSIONS

1 ▶ 6.1 Listen to a discussion about ways to generate electricity at a school. Read the topics and write *MT* (main topic) or *D* (digression).

1 Installing solar panels on the roof of the cafeteria _____
2 Popularity of solar panels in Europe _____
3 How much power solar panels can generate _____
4 Improved appearance of solar panels _____
5 Cost and reliability of solar panels _____
6 Government programs for energy-saving improvements to one's home _____
7 Installation and maintenance of solar panels _____
8 Keeping one's room clean _____

UNDERSTANDING PERSUASIVE TECHNIQUES

2 ▶ 6.1 Listen again. Match the persuasive techniques to the sentences from the discussion.

1 But how do you know how much power they produce? _____
2 OK, so I understand what Ezra's saying – and, yes, solar panels are being installed everywhere. But there are some problems with them. _____
3 They can't just be installed on a roof that's, I don't know, really old, or has leaks – and what's more, they need a lot of maintenance. _____
4 I know what you're saying, Gabriela, but trust me, it's not a lot of work to keep them clean. You don't have to worry about that. _____
5 I don't know. Don't you think it would be a pain to have to clean them all the time? _____

a adding information
b asking a question
c challenging a point
d expressing reservations
e reassuring

PART B PRONUNCIATION FOR LISTENING
INTONATION RELATED TO EMOTION

3 ▶ 6.2 Listen to the sentences. Label each sentence with a different emotion from the box.

annoyance	boredom	excitement	surprise	worry

1 Some of those government programs are awesome! _____
2 OK, Milo, that's great, but we're talking about generating power, not saving it. _____
3 If one of the elements goes bad, the whole system shuts down! What would you do then? _____
4 Whoa! I didn't know that! _____
5 I know what you're saying, Gabriela, but trust me, it's not a lot of work to keep them clean. _____

Name: _____   Date: _____

PART A KEY VOCABULARY

1   Complete the sentences with correct form of the words in the box.

| capacity   consumption   drawback   efficient   experimental   limitation   maintenance   network |

1   Our solar panels are connected to the electric company's _____ .
2   One _____ to geothermal systems is their high cost.
3   We're trying to limit our _____ of electricity by turning off lights and computers after office hours.
4   The new wind turbine has the _____ to produce enough electricity for 800 homes.
5   Most new appliances use less energy and are much more _____ than those used in the past.
6   This is a very conservative community. Most people aren't interested in _____ sources of energy.
7   The city has imposed a(n) _____ on the number of cars that can enter the downtown area in order to reduce traffic and pollution.
8   The _____ cost of the solar panels increased 12 percent last year due to damages from storms.

2   Complete the paragraphs with the correct form of the words in the box.

| consistent   cycle   element   function   generate   mainland   reservoir   volume |

Since ancient times, human beings have used hydropower – power produced by moving water. In the late nineteenth century, people began using hydropower to [1]_____ electricity, and hydroelectricity was born.
Most hydroelectric power plants have at least two [2]_____ : a(n) [3]_____ and a dam. The dam is like a huge door. Its [4]_____ is to control the flow of a large [5]_____ of water from, for instance, a river. Dams operate according to a [6]_____ that follows a(n) [7]_____ pattern: they close, and water fills up a large area, such as Lake Terra; they open, and the water rushes out. The force of the water powers a generator in the dam, which in turn produces electricity. The electricity produced by Lake Terra supplies our city, here on the [8]_____ , as well as the islands off the coast.

PART B LANGUAGE DEVELOPMENT
CONNECTING IDEAS BETWEEN SENTENCES

3 Choose the correct transition words or phrases to complete the sentences.

1 Solar power is not yet capable of generating large amounts of electricity. _____ , most energy companies believe it will be important in the near future.
   a Therefore   **b** Nevertheless   **c** What's more

2 Coal and oil are very harmful to the environment, _____ we need to invest in alternative sources of energy.
   a so   **b** in addition   **c** moreover

3 Nuclear power is a good source of cheap electricity. _____ , it can be extremely dangerous if an accident occurs.
   a Therefore   **b** As a result   **c** On the other hand

4 We want to use less electricity in our office. _____ , we would like you to turn off the lights when you leave a room.
   a In addition   **b** Therefore   **c** Nevertheless

5 Wind power can be one of the cheapest sources of renewable energy. _____ , it is not harmful to the environment.
   a Even so   **b** Furthermore   **c** As a result

THE PASSIVE VOICE

4 Read the sentences. Write *A* (active) or *P* (passive).

1 What sources of power could be used here? _____
2 They could generate all the power we need. _____
3 Yes, solar panels are being installed everywhere. _____
4 But there are some problems with them. _____
5 On cloudy days no electricity will be produced. _____
6 They can't just be installed on an old, leaky roof. _____

ACADEMIC VOCABULARY FOR NETWORKS AND SYSTEMS

5 Complete the paragraph with the correct form of the words in the box.

challenge	element	network	potential	source

With the cost of electricity rising every year, we face a(n) [1]_____ to find alternatives. We believe that installing a(n) [2]_____ of solar thermal panels on the roof of our building has the [3]_____ to save us hundreds of dollars a year. The [4]_____ of such a system are fairly simple: water is drawn from a(n) [5]_____ , such as a well, through the solar panels, where it is heated by the sun. That hot water then returns to a storage tank in the basement.

Name: _____ Date: _____

PART A KEY SKILLS
DISTINGUISHING FACT FROM OPINION

1 ▶ 7.1 Listen to a radio show about a new art exhibit in a museum. Are these statements facts or opinions? Write *F* (fact) or *O* (opinion).

1 Pedro is a well-known art critic who works for the Metropolitan Museum of Art in New York City. _____
2 As you can see, the similarities are absolutely remarkable! _____
3 Here, for example, we have a print of Van Gogh's famous painting *The Starry Night*. _____
4 Everyone will immediately recognize this masterpiece. _____
5 Both works make us feel calm. _____
6 The bird is a little strange, wouldn't you say? _____
7 I interpret the bird as a symbol of life, and hope! _____
8 And now I'd like to talk to Evelyn Shoemaker, who is visiting from Peoria, Illinois. _____
9 I think art is such an important form of self-expression, don't you? _____
10 Evelyn is pointing to a large print of Mark Rothko's famous painting *Orange and Yellow*, which he did in 1961. _____

INFERRING OPINIONS

2 ▶ 7.2 Listen to the excerpts from the radio show. What is the speaker really saying? Circle the correct inference.

1 I'm not sure I see what the similarities are between these two pieces.
   a The two pieces are similar.
   b The two pieces are different.
2 Yes, but, the sky in Van Gogh's painting has brilliant colors – those blues and yellows and white – whereas the sky in the boy's painting is just black.
   a The boy's painting is much less sophisticated than Van Gogh's.
   b The boy's painting uses color well.
3 As several critics have commented, he has drawn both a moon and a sun, and a bird.
   a The boy's painting is realistic.
   b The boy's painting is absurd.
4 Well, this area looks like it could be the sea, and these lines remind me of a horse.
   a The woman recognizes the objects in the painting.
   b The woman thinks it's not important to recognize the objects in the painting.
5 I'm not sure you need to think too much about what the picture reveals.
   a You shouldn't think too much about what a painting is communicating.
   b Good art should reveal something that's true.

PART B PRONUNCIATION FOR LISTENING
STRESS IN WORD FAMILIES

2 ▶ 7.3 Listen and underline the stressed syllables in each word pair.

1 exhibit   exhibition
2 compose   composition
3 interpret   interpretation
4 express   expression
5 similar   similarity
6 symbol   symbolic

Name: _____ Date: _____

PART A KEY VOCABULARY

1 Read the sentences. Match the definitions to the words in bold.

1 This is a very difficult subject that I do not wish to **comment** on at this time. _____
2 Today we are going to **analyze** the use of color in Rivera's paintings. _____
3 When we talk about the **composition** of a painting, we are referring to how the visual elements or objects are arranged. _____
4 These children have shown great **creativity** in using the materials they have to produce amazing art. _____
5 We greatly **appreciate** your donation to the museum. _____
6 Some artists don't want to display their works because they are afraid of **criticism**. _____
7 And now, we're going to **reveal** the name of the artist who created this work: Jorge Salinas! _____
8 Some people **focus on** the details of a work of art and don't see the big picture. _____

a to show something that was previously hidden or secret
b to study something in a systematic and careful way
c a careful discussion of something in order to judge its quality or explain its meaning
d to express an opinion
e to give a lot of attention to one particular person, subject, or thing
f the way that people or things are arranged in a painting or photograph
g to recognize how good or useful something is
h the ability to produce original and unusual ideas, or to make something new or imaginative

2 Complete the sentences with the correct form of the words in the box.

| display   identity   interpret   reject   remove   restore   right   self-expression |

1 We have hired experts to _____ the damaged paintings to their original condition.
2 The artist never used his real name, so we may never know his true _____ .
3 In this country everyone has a(n) _____ to say what they think.
4 Graffiti artists _____ the idea that paintings belong only in museums.
5 The school encourages _____ from its students through the arts, including painting, sculpture, and music.
6 I _____ the dark cloud in her painting to mean that something bad is going to happen.
7 The artists hope to _____ their works for everyone to see in the library next week.
8 I want to _____ some photos so that I have more memory on my phone. How do I do this?

PART B LANGUAGE DEVELOPMENT
RELATIVE CLAUSES

3 Complete the sentences with the correct relative pronoun in parentheses. Then underline the noun that each relative clause refers to.

1 I'm joined by Pedro Salinas, _____ works for the Metropolitan Museum. (who / whose / which)
2 The show _____ opened last Tuesday features works by famous artists and children. (who / that / whose)
3 Tim, a boy _____ lives in Cleveland, Ohio, painted this picture. (that / which / who)
4 She is pointing to Rothko's famous painting *Orange and Yellow*, _____ he did in 1961. (whose / which / who)
5 The artist, _____ works are on display at the City Museum, grew up in a small town in Ohio. (which / whose / that)

Name: _____ Date: _____

PART A KEY SKILLS
UNDERSTANDING SPECIFIC OBSERVATIONS AND GENERALIZATIONS

1 ▶ 8.1 Listen to a radio show about an active adult community. Then read the statements from the show and write G (generalization) or S (specific observation).

1 Oh, it varies, but mainly we're talking about people 55 years and older. _____

2 The older generation is really different these days. _____

3 My grandparents, for instance, love doing things. They both like to golf, and my grandfather manages to play tennis at least twice a week. _____

4 Most people actually prefer living in their own homes. They just don't want the responsibility of taking care of all the outdoor work and repairs. _____

5 Well, I know that my parents refuse to sell their house anytime soon. _____

6 I mean, too often if a gym or pool is crowded or hard to get to, people just give up and never go. _____

7 I know that I won't go to the gym at the end of the day anymore – between about 6 and 8 – because it's just too busy. _____

8 Everyone loves our cultural offerings! _____

9 I'm sure they're a big hit with the residents. _____

10 I'm going to devote my time to learning Chinese and bird-watching and ... _____

PART B PRONUNCIATION FOR LISTENING
CONSONANT REDUCTIONS AND JOINED VOWELS

2 ▶ 8.2 Listen to the sentences. Check the correct description for the words in bold.

	vowels joined with /y/	vowels joined with /w/	dropped /d/	dropped /t/
1 **What do you** mean by the term "active adult community"?				
2 So, at Sun Village we **want to** attract people who can live on their own.				
3 Oh, we offer single-family homes, **and then** of course we have condominiums.				
4 Wow, that's amazing. Sorry – **go on**.				
5 I mean, **too often** if a gym or pool is crowded or hard to get to, people just give up and never go.				
6 I know I won't go to the gym at **the end** of the day anymore.				

Name: _____   Date: _____

PART A KEY VOCABULARY

1 Read the sentences and circle the correct definition for the words in bold.

1 At Sun Village we want to attract people who can live on their own, but who also want to live – and **participate** – in a vibrant community.
   a exist
   b become involved
   c invest

2 Recent research **indicates** that the market for this kind of community is huge!
   a proves
   b explains
   c shows, points, or makes clear in another way

3 You know, the older **generation** is really different these days.
   a all of the people of about the same age within a society or within a particular family
   b a group of people from one part of a country
   c men and women below the age of 50

4 They just don't want the **responsibility** of taking care of all the outdoor work and repairs.
   a duty to take care of someone or something
   b cost of doing something
   c effort to accomplish something

5 I mean, the **property** is enormous – over 800 acres.
   a area
   b community
   c land and buildings owned by someone

6 We want to **ensure** that people can remain active.
   a make a promise to someone
   b make something certain to happen
   c permit someone to do something

7 I know that I, for one, cannot wait for **retirement**.
   a the point at which someone stops working, especially because of having reached a particular age
   b a period of relaxation or vacation due to stress at work
   c old age

8 I'm going to **devote** my time to learning Chinese and bird-watching.
   a forget to do something
   b avoid doing something
   c use time, energy, etc. for a particular purpose

2 Complete the sentences with the correct form of the words in the box.

ancestor   asset   contribute   dependent   institution   pension   permit   provider

1 My parents would rather spend their old age in their own home than move to a(n) _____ for the elderly.
2 Their grandparents signed over many of their _____ , including their home, to their children after they retired.
3 The school _____ retirees to take classes for free, while others must pay for them.
4 Ana, who is 51, has three _____ living with her: a son and two grandchildren.
5 I would love to visit Ireland to see where my _____ lived 100 years ago.
6 People who do not have a(n) _____ should invest in a private retirement plan.
7 The number of women who are the sole _____ for their families has increased in recent years.
8 Wilson always _____ 15% of his paycheck to a long-term savings plan.

PART B LANGUAGE DEVELOPMENT
VERBS WITH INFINITIVES OR GERUNDS

3 Correct the mistakes in the sentences.

1 Many people are concerned about what they are going do when they retire.

2 It's important to start save for retirement when you are young.

3 His financial coach convinced him to opening a retirement savings account.

4 We've noticed that many older people like to living in a warmer climate.

5 Perhaps you'd consider to buy an apartment in the city.

UNIT 1 LISTENING QUIZ
PART A KEY SKILLS

1 1 b 2 c 3 b 4 a 5 c

PART B ADDITIONAL SKILLS

2 1 T
   2 F; Overseas sales of American films have skyrocketed in recent years.
   3 F; China is the second-largest market for American films.
   4 F; China allows 34 films to be imported every year.
   5 T

PART C PRONUNCIATION FOR LISTENING

3 1 airplane, contribute 2 produced, profitable
   3 comprehend, influence 4 sixth
   5 strengths, worldwide

UNIT 1 LANGUAGE QUIZ
PART A KEY VOCABULARY

1 1 overseas 2 agriculture 3 source 4 domestic
   5 transportation 6 consumer
   7 importing / to import 8 processed

2 1 produce / produced 2 greenhouse
   3 investigating 4 purchase 5 exported
   6 households

PART B LANGUAGE DEVELOPMENT

3 1 can't have been grown 2 must have arrived
   3 could have bought 4 must be imported
   5 might have been made

4 1 climate change 2 carbon footprint
   3 carbon emissions 4 processing 5 supply chain

UNIT 2 LISTENING QUIZ
PART A KEY SKILLS

1 1 b 2 a 3 b

2 2, 5

PART B ADDITIONAL SKILLS

3 1 universities 2 free 3 students 4 Some
   5 positive

PART C PRONUNCIATION FOR LISTENING

4 1 U 2 C 3 U 4 C 5 U

UNIT 2 LANGUAGE QUIZ
PART A KEY VOCABULARY

1 1 mechanical 2 understanding 3 complex
   4 practical 5 manual 6 academic 7 vocational
   8 specialist

2 1 medical 2 internship 3 professional 4 acquire
   5 advisor 6 physical 7 secure 8 technical

PART B LANGUAGE DEVELOPMENT

3 1 prefer to 2 live 3 studying 4 to travel
   5 work

UNIT 3 LISTENING QUIZ
PART A KEY SKILLS

1 1 DC 2 DM 3 DC 4 DM 5 DM

2 1 d 2 a 3 c 4 b 5 e

PART B PRONUNCIATION FOR LISTENING

3 1 U 2 U 3 A 4 A 5 A 6 A

UNIT 3 LANGUAGE QUIZ
PART A KEY VOCABULARY

1 1 outbreak 2 occurred 3 contracted
   4 precautions 5 treatment 6 data 7 infected
   8 recovered 9 clinical 10 trials

2 1 researcher 2 scientific 3 factors 4 controlled
   5 prove 6 prevention

PART B LANGUAGE DEVELOPMENT

3 1 d 2 e 3 a 4 b 5 c

4 1 If the polio vaccine had existed in the 1940s, my grandmother would not <u>have gotten</u> the disease.
   2 If we had taken our malaria pills, we <u>wouldn't have become</u> so sick.
   3 Noah's infection <u>could have been</u> cured if we had had the proper antibiotics.
   4 If people practice preventative medicine, they <u>could avoid</u> many illnesses.
   5 If everyone got the flu vaccine, there <u>would be</u> fewer outbreaks in the coming year.

UNIT 4 LISTENING QUIZ
PART A KEY SKILLS

1 1 a, b   2 d, e   3 b

2 1 a   2 d   3 e   4 c   5 b

PART B PRONUNCIATION FOR LISTENING

3 1 What he found in this <u>wild</u>, lonely area was <u>trash</u>: miles and miles of <u>plastic waste</u>.
  2 No matter <u>what</u> time of day I looked, <u>plastic debris</u> was floating <u>everywhere</u>.
  3 Do the actions of <u>one</u> person <u>really impact</u> the <u>world</u>?
  4 Now, the <u>problem</u> with plastic is that it does <u>not biodegrade</u>.
  5 The plastic waste is breaking down into <u>tiny</u> pieces, full of <u>toxic</u> chemicals, that marine animals are <u>eating</u>.
  6 There really is <u>no way</u> for these animals to <u>adapt</u> to changes like these in their environment.

UNIT 4 LANGUAGE QUIZ
PART A KEY VOCABULARY

1 1 conservation   2 habitat   3 coastal   4 impact
  5 adapt   6 modified   7 waste   8 exploit
  9 wilderness

2 1 f   2 a   3 e   4 b   5 c   6 d

PART B LANGUAGE DEVELOPMENT

3 1 to   2 to   3 from   4 with   5 in

4 1 had finished   2 had decided   3 had ever gone
  4 had found   5 had discovered

5 1 affect   2 declined   3 adapt   4 exploited
  5 survive

UNIT 5 LISTENING QUIZ
PART A GENERAL SKILLS

1 1 c   2 e   3 d   4 a   5 b

PART B KEY SKILLS

2 1 Paradise on Earth   2 a huge umbrella   3 in a tree house   4 as much as a Tesla   5 on a cloud

3 1 S   2 T   3 S   4 S   5 S

PART C PRONUNCIATION FOR LISTENING

4 1 A: I'm sorry, but won't that make the house pretty <u>dark inside</u>?

  B: <u>Actually</u>, we anticipate that the inside will receive <u>adequate sunlight</u> during the day to do <u>most</u> things.

  2 A: Yes, but solar panels are really <u>expensive</u>. I mean, only <u>rich</u> people can really <u>afford</u> them.

  B: But we believe that solar is a <u>great investment</u> in a home... . I think solar power will become more <u>common everywhere</u>.

UNIT 5 LANGUAGE QUIZ
PART A KEY VOCABULARY

1 1 concerned   2 existing   3 adequate   4 anticipate
  5 appropriate   6 ambitious   7 investment
  8 potential

2 1 obtain   2 transformed   3 collapse   4 features
  5 sympathetic   6 contemporary   7 controversial

PART B LANGUAGE DEVELOPMENT

3 1 We're **definitely** going to see a game in the new arena this summer.
  2 They're **probably** going to replace the old windows with new ones this fall.
  3 **Maybe** my parents will move to a smaller house someday.
  4 I **certainly** won't live in an apartment without air conditioning.
  5 **Perhaps** we'll have enough money one day to build a new garage.

4 1 transformed   2 abandoned   3 converted
  4 anticipates   5 maintain   6 expand

UNIT 6 LISTENING QUIZ
PART A KEY SKILLS

1 1 MT   2 D   3 MT   4 D   5 MT   6 D   7 MT
  8 D

2 1 b   2 c   3 a   4 e   5 d

PART B PRONUNCIATION FOR LISTENING

3 1 excitement   2 annoyance   3 fear   4 surprise
  5 boredom

UNIT 6 LANGUAGE QUIZ
PART A KEY VOCABULARY

1 1 network 2 drawback 3 consumption
4 capacity 5 efficient 6 experimental
7 limitation 8 maintenance

2 1 generate 2 elements 3 reservoir 4 function
5 volume 6 cycle 7 consistent 8 mainland

PART B LANGUAGE DEVELOPMENT

3 1 b 2 a 3 c 4 b 5 b

4 1 P 2 A 3 P 4 A 5 P 6 P

5 1 challenge 2 network 3 potential 4 elements
5 source

UNIT 7 LISTENING QUIZ
PART A KEY SKILLS

1 1 F 2 O 3 F 4 O 5 O 6 O 7 O 8 F
9 O 10 F

2 1 b 2 a 3 b 4 b 5 a

PART B PRONUNCIATION FOR LISTENING

3 1 ex<u>hi</u>bit   exhi<u>bi</u>tion
2 com<u>pose</u>   compo<u>si</u>tion
3 in<u>ter</u>pret   interpre<u>ta</u>tion
4 ex<u>press</u>   ex<u>pre</u>ssion
5 <u>si</u>milar   simi<u>la</u>rity
6 <u>sym</u>bol   sym<u>bo</u>lic

UNIT 7 LANGUAGE QUIZ
PART A KEY VOCABULARY

1 1 d 2 b 3 f 4 h 5 g 6 c 7 a 8 e

2 1 restore 2 identity 3 right 4 reject / rejected /
have rejected 5 self-expression 6 interpret /
interpreted 7 display 8 remove

PART B LANGUAGE DEVELOPMENT

3 1 who, <u>Pedro Salinas</u> 2 that, <u>show</u>
3 who, <u>boy</u> 4 which, <u>painting</u> / <u>*Orange and Yellow*</u>
5 whose, <u>artist</u>

UNIT 8 LISTENING QUIZ
PART A KEY SKILLS

1 1 S 2 G 3 S 4 G 5 S 6 G 7 S 8 G
9 G 10 S

PART B PRONUNCIATION FOR LISTENING

2 1 dropped /t/
2 dropped /t/
3 dropped /d/
4 vowels joined with /w/
5 vowels joined with /w/
6 vowels joined with /y/

UNIT 8 LANGUAGE QUIZ
PART A KEY VOCABULARY

1 1 b 2 c 3 a 4 a 5 c 6 b 7 a 8 c

2 1 institution 2 assets 3 permits 4 dependents
5 ancestors 6 pension 7 providers
8 contributes

PART B LANGUAGE DEVELOPMENT

3 1 Many people are concerned about what they are
going <u>to</u> do when they retire.
2 It's important to start ~~save~~ saving for retirement
when you are young.
3 His financial coach convinced him to ~~opening~~ <u>open</u>
a retirement savings account.
4 We've noticed that many older people like ~~to~~ living
in a warmer climate. / We've noticed that many
older people like to ~~living~~ <u>live</u> in a warmer climate.
5 Perhaps you'd consider ~~to buy~~ <u>buying</u> an apartment
in the city.

UNIT 1

🔊 **1.1**

Oscar: So, we've discussed how globalization has affected several industries, including agriculture and consumer electronics. We've looked at how transportation of these products between the source and the consumer is a key factor for those industries, and how it may be contributing to, among other things, climate change. But today I'd like to investigate how globalization is affecting another industry, one that is near and dear to most of us: the film industry. We'll start with a look at the U.S. film industry, centered in Hollywood, California. Let's welcome an expert in this topic, Gabriela Chan. Ms. Chan, thank you so much for joining us today.

Gabriela: Oh, thank you! It's really a pleasure to be here. So, um, how do I begin? Well, everyone knows that Hollywood produces hugely profitable movies, but not everyone is aware of how much these American studios make in overseas sales. Those numbers have skyrocketed in recent years, and they're changing the way films are made.

Oscar: Could you give us any examples?

Gabriela: Oh, of course! If you'll look at these two pie charts, you'll see that the first one shows what the top 5 Hollywood movies of 2016 earned in terms of domestic sales. Now compare that with the second chart, which shows what those same five movies grossed overseas. Now, do you notice a pattern?

Oscar: That's amazing! It looks as though they all earned more overseas. Is that possible?

Gabriela: Absolutely! Take, for example, the number one movie in terms of sales for 2016, *Captain America: Civil War*. That movie grossed $408 million in the U.S., but as an export, it brought in over $744 million!

Oscar: Well, that's just phenomenal! And even if we look at the movie that earned the least overseas …

Gabriela: Yes, that would be *Deadpool*, number five on both charts.

Oscar: Well, it still earned more overseas than it did in the U.S.

Gabriela: Yes. Amazing, isn't it? So, this shift in sales from a predominantly domestic market to an overseas one is changing the way these studios do business. China, for example, is now the second-largest market for U.S. films. However, China has laws about importing films: it only allows 34 foreign films into the country every year.

Oscar: So, what are American film studios doing?

Gabriela: Well, for one, some are co-producing movies in China with local studios. For example, *Kung Fu Panda 3*, which was one of the top twenty movies of the year, was animated in California and Shanghai at the same time. And it was co-produced by an American company, DreamWorks, and its Asian spinoff, Oriental DreamWorks.

Oscar: Well, that's certainly clever, isn't it? So DreamWorks is truly a global company now.

🔊 **1.2**

1. How does airplane travel contribute to climate change?
2. Hollywood produced the ten most profitable movies last year.
3. It's difficult to comprehend the amount of influence they have on the industry.
4. Edmonton is the sixth largest city in Canada by population.
5. One of Hollywood's strengths is producing successful blockbusters worldwide.

UNIT 2

🔊 **2.1**

Anna: So, Jake, have you decided yet what you want to do when you graduate?

Jake: Well, I'd like to go to college, but I don't know what I really want to do – you know, for a career. I guess I could start by taking a class or two – but I can't really ask my parents to pay for a course that's not very practical.

Anna: Have you thought about a MOOC? A Massive Open Online Course? They're online courses run by universities, so you can study from home, whenever you want.

Jake: Yeah, but I'd rather not spend a lot of money right now …

Anna: No, that's the great thing: MOOCs are usually free – and anybody can sign up for one. There are often thousands or even hundreds of thousands of students signed up for each course!

Jake: Wow! Sounds good. But … So how do the universities cover their costs?

Anna: Er … I'm not sure. Maybe they sell advertising on their website … I mean, if thousands of people visit their website every day, they could make a lot of money.

Jake: Hmm ... But there must be some costs, right? If you write an essay, don't they need to pay a professor to grade it?

Anna: No, students check and grade each other's work. The university tells you how to do it. I think it works pretty well.

Jake: I don't know. It sounds pretty complex to me. I think I'd rather go to a real school – you know, an actual, physical place – rather than doing everything online. But ... what kinds of courses do they offer?

Anna: Oh, everything!

Jake: But do they offer classes in any technical subjects – like, you know, engineering or computer science?

Anna: Uh, I'm sure they do ... You should google "MOOCs" and see what's out there. I do know that some of the top schools, like Harvard and MIT, offer MOOCs.

Jake: Wow, really – Harvard? I'd really like to take a course from Harvard ...

Anna: Then you ought to visit their website and see what they're offering! You might find a class you really like.

Jake: OK, OK. I will. Thanks for the suggestion!

🔊 2.2

1 I guess I could start by taking a class or two.
2 No, that's the great thing: MOOCs are usually free.
3 But there must be some costs, right?
4 The university tells you how to do it. I think it works pretty well.
5 I don't know. It sounds pretty complex to me.

UNIT 3

🔊 3.1

Host: Hello, and welcome to *Your Health Today!* Our topic this evening is homeopathy, an alternative system of medicine. What is it? Does it work? With us today are Dr. Amelia Cooper, a homeopathic doctor in Connecticut, and Dr. Ethan Martinez of University Hospital in Chicago. To begin: Dr. Cooper, could you please explain to us what homeopathy is?

Dr. Cooper: Yes, sure, of course. Homeopathy – which was created in 1696, in Germany – is based on the fact that "like cures like" – that the substance that makes healthy people sick can, sometimes, make a sick person better.

Dr. Martinez: Excuse me, but I believe homeopathy began in 1796, not 1696, didn't it?

Dr. Cooper: Oh, yes, you're right: it was 1796 ... . At any rate, homeopathic medicines contain tiny amounts of active substances that in larger amounts would cause a problem. If a person is suffering from hay fever, for

example, a homeopathic treatment containing red onion, which usually causes people's eyes to tear and their noses to run, can actually help them. The body senses the onion in the medicine, but the amount is so small, and the body's defense reaction so strong, that the overall effect is to help the person recover from their illness. It's a powerful principle, don't you think?

Host: Thank you, Dr. Cooper, thank you. ... Dr. Martinez, I understand that you are not a big supporter of homeopathy, are you? Could you tell us what you think of Dr. Cooper's statement?

Dr. Martinez: Well, to me her homeopathic treatment sounds pretty simple, doesn't it? However, in reality there is little scientific data to support it. In fact, again and again clinical trials have shown that homeopathic medicines are *placebos*. A placebo is a false medicine that does nothing. When researchers test a new medicine, they give half the people in the test a placebo – often a sugar tablet – so that they can see if the real medicine actually works. Dr. Cooper mentioned that homeopathic medicines contain tiny amounts of active substances, but she didn't say just how tiny, did she? One popular homeopathic medicine, for example, is made from pure water! I don't believe most people think water is a medicine, do they?

Host: Dr. Cooper?

Dr. Cooper: First of all, I've heard these arguments many times before. In my opinion, just because scientists don't yet understand exactly how homeopathy works doesn't prove that it's wrong, does it? In my practice, I've personally seen hundreds of people who have benefited from homeopathic remedies.

Dr. Martinez: Oh, I'd have to disagree. I believe that most scientists do understand homeopathy, as I've just explained. Homeopaths make extraordinary claims about their placebo medicines because it's a good way of making money. This is a multi-million dollar industry after all, isn't it? In fact it seems to me to be an industry in which people sell sugar and water at ridiculous prices to people who need real medical help. It is extremely dangerous ...

Host: Wow! Strong opinions from both sides there.

🔊 3.2

1 Excuse me, but I believe homeopathy began in 1796, not 1696, didn't it?
2 It's a powerful principle, don't you think?
3 Well, to me her homeopathic treatment sounds pretty simple, doesn't it?
4 Dr. Cooper mentioned that homeopathic medicines contain tiny amounts of active substances, but she didn't say just how tiny, did she?

5 Just because scientists don't yet understand exactly how homeopathy works doesn't prove that it's wrong, does it?

6 This is a multi-million dollar industry after all, isn't it?

UNIT 4

🔊 4.1

Speaker: About 20 years ago – in early 1997 – a man named Charles Moore was sailing home across the North Pacific Ocean. He had finished a sailing race and was heading back from Hawaii to Santa Barbara, California. Rather than taking the usual route, he had decided to take a thousand-mile "shortcut" through a high-pressure area in the central Pacific Ocean, where few people had ever gone.

What he found in this wild, lonely area was trash: miles and miles of plastic waste. As he reported, "In the week it took to cross the subtropical high, no matter what time of day I looked, plastic debris was floating everywhere: bottles, bottle caps, wrappers … parts of TVs, volleyballs, truck tires." Based on what he had found, he calculated the total weight of the trash to be about three million tons.

The area Moore had discovered is now called the Great Pacific Garbage Patch, or GPGP. It stretches from the coastal waters of California to the shores of Japan. It is growing so quickly that, according to Jacqueline McGlade, a scientist from the UN Environment Programme, "It is beginning to be seen from outer space, like the Great Wall of China."

Now, it's important to understand that the oceans of the world flow in a series of circles thousands of miles wide due to wind patterns, as well as the rotation of the planet. The GPGP lies in the center of one of the largest circles. Currents from four different corners of the world circle around this area. Waste is pulled into the center, which is relatively calm.

Now, you might sometimes ask yourself, "how can what I do really affect the environment? Do the actions of one person really impact the world?" Well, let's consider this: one person throws a plastic water bottle into the ocean near Los Angeles, for example. The California Current catches that bottle and carries it south toward Mexico. There, another current – the North Equatorial Current – carries it all the way across the vast Pacific Ocean, to the shores of Japan. The currents circling around the Great Pacific Garbage Patch then gradually draw the bottle into the center, where it is trapped. Now, the problem with plastic is that it does not biodegrade. It is not natural – it is man-made. Instead of breaking down into elements like carbon and oxygen that living beings can use, a plastic water bottle will

eventually break down into smaller pieces, owing to the forces of wind and water and sunlight – but those pieces will always be plastic. Plastic survives.

And this is one of the biggest problems with this sea of plastic known as the Great Pacific Garbage Patch: the plastic waste is breaking down into tiny pieces, full of toxic chemicals, that marine animals are eating. Birds see these bits of plastic and think they are fish eggs, and they eat them or feed them to their young, who then die from starvation. These tiny bits of plastic form larger masses that all kinds of marine life – seals and turtles and fish, for example – swim into, and become trapped and die. There really is no way for these animals to adapt to changes like these in their environment.

So, what can we do to solve this problem? How can we clean up the GPGP? One promising idea is to use a series of connected platforms to collect the waste. The platforms could be made of wood or, better yet, metal. The ocean's own currents should push the waste toward these platforms, where it can be extracted and recycled. If this idea worked, something exciting would occur: the whole area could be cleaned within five years, and possibly even at a profit.

Let's look more closely now at this idea …

🔊 4.2

1 What he found in this wild, lonely area was trash: miles and miles of plastic waste.

2 No matter what time of day I looked, plastic debris was floating everywhere.

3 Do the actions of one person really impact the world?

4 Now, the problem with plastic is that it does not biodegrade.

5 The plastic waste is breaking down into tiny pieces, full of toxic chemicals, that marine animals are eating.

6 There really is no way for these animals to adapt to changes like these in their environment.

UNIT 5

 5.1

Teacher: We've been looking at examples of green buildings – buildings that are both energy-efficient and environmentally conscious – around the world. Today we're going to hear from Rafa Morales, the lead architect of a green building company in Costa Rica. Mr. Morales?

Rafa: Yes, thank you, thank you. As you probably know, Costa Rica is famous for its amazing natural beauty – some people call Costa Rica "Paradise on Earth." In Costa Rica, we value both beauty and the environment, so it will probably not surprise many of you to learn that Costa Rica is a world leader in green buildings.

Today I'd like to present you with the designs for some very exciting homes we'll be building in Costa Rica in the next few years. This first slide shows our design for a house we're going to build in Malpais, on the Pacific coast. As you can see, the house will definitely have a contemporary look, with its glass walls and natural colors.

Student 1: Excuse me, but isn't it really hot in that part of the country?

Rafa: Well, yes. Some months are hotter than others, but we've planned for that. I'd like to draw your attention to the roof – and to the porch, which is going to wrap around the entire house. Do you see how far the roof extends? This will shade the porch like a huge umbrella during the hottest part of the day. And it's going to make the inside of the home significantly cooler.

Student 2: I'm sorry, but won't that make the house pretty dark inside?

Rafa: An excellent question. Actually, we anticipate that the inside will receive adequate sunlight during the day to do most things – to read, to cook – without using lights. The glass blocks that we're going to use in the walls and ceilings will bring sunlight into all corners of the house, while maintaining structural support.

Student 3: And what do the porches do?

Rafa: Ah, I'm glad you asked that. These porches are one of my favorite features. They will greatly expand the existing living space of the house. This house will be surrounded by tropical trees. Just imagine: sitting on this porch will be like sitting in a tree house.

Student 1: What sources of energy will these houses use, and will they save people money?

Rafa: Another great question! As it happens, we have some very ambitious plans for solar ...

Student 1: Yes, but solar panels are really expensive. They cost as much as a Tesla! I mean, only rich people can really afford them.

Rafa: Well, you have a point. Solar power is still a little controversial – the panels can be a bit expensive at the moment. But we believe that solar is a great investment in a home. I think that in the next few years we're going to see some dramatic changes. I think solar power will become more common everywhere, and that will make it much more affordable.

Student 2: Will all your houses have just one floor?

Rafa: Well, yes, these first houses will have one main floor. But, as you can see in this slide, the ceilings will be very high, contributing to the overall feeling of floating on air. Several of our homes will have a loft

space, which can be used for storage – or you could convert it into a spare bedroom for guests. Sleeping in one of these lofts would be like sleeping on a cloud.

🔊 5.2

1 As you can see, the house will definitely have a contemporary look, with its glass walls and natural colors.

2 Excuse me, but isn't it really hot in that part of the country?

3 And it's going to make the inside of the home significantly cooler.

4 They will greatly expand the existing living space of the house.

5 I think that in the next few years we're going to see some dramatic changes.

🔊 5.3

1 A: I'm sorry, but won't that make the house pretty dark inside?

   B: Actually, we anticipate that the inside will receive adequate sunlight during the day to do most things.

2 A: Yes, but solar panels are really expensive. I mean, only rich people can really afford them.

   B: But we believe that solar is a great investment in a home ... I think solar power will become more common everywhere.

UNIT 6

🔊 6.1

Professor: Alright, so, last week I presented all of you with a challenge: to think of ways in which electricity could be generated right here at the college. What are some sources of power that could be used here? What are the strengths and limitations of those systems? OK, so, Ezra, you seem to have some ideas ...

Ezra: Yes, thanks, I do. Um, well, I think almost all our needs could be met by installing solar panels on the roof of the cafeteria. There's plenty of space for them there, and they could generate all the power we'd need. I've heard they're becoming really popular in Europe.

Professor: OK, great. But how do you know how much power they produce?

Ezra: Oh, because I looked into it! I mean, just one solar panel has the capacity to produce 200 watts of electricity. And, um, when a bunch of panels are all connected – you know, like on a roof – well, that network of panels can generate a ton of power. Plus, they're making panels that are a lot better looking than the old ones.

Gabriela: OK, so I understand what Ezra's saying – and, yes, solar panels are being installed everywhere. But there are some problems with them. I mean, they can be really expensive, and they only work when it's really sunny. So, that means that on cloudy days no electricity will be produced.

Ezra: OK, but solar panels are getting cheaper all the time – and also there are a lot of government programs that help people pay for them.

Milo: Yeah, that's true. Some of those government programs are awesome! You can get money from the government for other energy-saving things you do to your house, like putting in new windows.

Professor: OK, Milo, that's great, but we're talking about generating power, not saving it.

Gabriela: You know, there's another drawback to solar panels: you have to have a really good roof to put them on. They can't just be installed on a roof that's, I don't know, really old, or has leaks – and what's more, they need a lot of maintenance. They have to be kept clean, and, um, if one of the elements goes bad, the whole system shuts down! What would you do then?

Milo: Whoa! I didn't know that!

Ezra: I know what you're saying, Gabriela, but trust me, it's not a lot of work to keep them clean. You don't have to worry about that.

Milo: I don't know. Don't you think it would be a pain to have to clean them all the time? I know I don't even like cleaning my room.

Professor: Well, Milo, I'd like to get back to talking about sources of energy. So, one question I have about solar panels is: how efficient are they these days? Are solar panels the best source of power available to us right now?

🔊 6.2

1 Some of those government programs are awesome!
2 OK, Milo, that's great, but we're talking about generating power, not saving it.
3 If one of the elements goes bad, the whole system shuts down! What would you do then?
4 Whoa! I didn't know that!
5 I know what you're saying, Gabriela, but trust me, it's not a lot of work to keep them clean.

UNIT 7

🔊 7.1

Abigail: Hello, and welcome to Art in America. I'm Abigail Vega, and today we're visiting the Institute of Contemporary Art in Chicago to see the show *The Creativity of Children*, which opened last Tuesday. I'm joined now by Pedro Salinas. Pedro is a well-known art critic who works for the Metropolitan Museum of Art in New York City. Mr. Salinas, could you tell us about the paintings in this exhibit?

Pedro: Yes, certainly, I'd be happy to. So, well, in this exhibit, a famous painting by a well-known artist – well, actually, a print of the painting – is displayed alongside a painting of a similar subject that was painted by a child. As you can see, the similarities are absolutely remarkable! Here, for example, we have a print of Van Gogh's famous painting *The Starry Night*. Everyone will immediately recognize this masterpiece. And beside it, a painting of a similar scene by Tim Chung, an eight-year-old boy who lives in Cleveland, Ohio.

Abigail: Um, OK, but I'm not sure I see what the similarities are between these two pieces. Perhaps you could help us analyze them.

Pedro: Oh, of course, of course. Well, as you can see, they are both scenes of a town at night, and both works make us feel calm. The composition of the two paintings is very similar – in both, you have a large tree in the front, the town behind it, and a large, dramatic night sky. We immediately focus on that sky.

Abigail: Yes, but, the sky in Van Gogh's painting has brilliant colors – those blues and yellows and white – whereas the sky in the boy's painting is just … black. And, as several critics have commented, he has drawn both a moon and a sun, and a bird. The bird is a little strange, wouldn't you say?

Pedro: Oh, no, not at all! In fact, I interpret the bird as a symbol of life, and hope!

Abigail: Right, I see. OK, thank you, Mr. Salinas. We appreciate your insights. Now I'd like to talk to Evelyn Shoemaker, who is visiting from Peoria, Illinois. Ms. Shoemaker, would you like to comment on this exhibition?

Evelyn: Oh, I'd be delighted to! But please, call me Evelyn! You know, I think art is such an important form of self-expression for young people today, don't you?

Abigail: Um, yes, sure. So, uh, do you have a favorite pair of paintings in this exhibit?

Evelyn: Yes, yes I do! I love this one!

Abigail: For our listeners: Ms. Shoemaker – er, Evelyn – is pointing to a large print of Mark Rothko's famous painting *Orange and Yellow*, which he did in 1961. And next to it is a work by nine-year-old Tanya Carter in which she's painted two big squares, one green and one blue. Could I ask you, Evelyn, why you chose these two?

Evelyn: Oh, I just love the colors! They make me feel good and they're very relaxing.

Abigail: And what do you see when you look at the pictures?

Evelyn: Well, this area looks like it could be the sea, and these lines remind me of a horse.

Abigail: A green horse? In the sea? Really?

Evelyn: Well now, I'm not sure you need to think too much about what the picture reveals. It's more about how it makes you feel, don't you think?

Abigail: OK, well then: thank you so much for your time, Ms. Shoemaker.

🔊 7.2

1 I'm not sure I see what the similarities are between these two pieces.

2 Yes, but, the sky in Van Gogh's painting has brilliant colors – those blues and yellows and white – whereas the sky in the boy's painting is just black.

3 As several critics have commented, he has drawn both a moon and a sun, and a bird.

4 Well, this area looks like it could be the sea, and these lines remind me of a horse.

5 I'm not sure you need to think too much about what the picture reveals.

🔊 7.3

1	exhibit	exhibition
2	compose	composition
3	interpret	interpretation
4	express	expression
5	similar	similarity
6	symbol	symbolic

UNIT 8

🔊 8.1

Noah: Hello, and welcome to *Aging in America*. Today we have with us the founders of Sun Village, a new active adult community in Arizona. Let me welcome Rosa Gonzales and Eric Stratford. Ms. Gonzalez, let me begin with you: what do you mean by the term "active adult community"?

Rosa: Well, basically, by "active" we mean independent. So, at Sun Village we want to attract people who can live on their own, but who also want to live – and participate – in a vibrant community. And recent research indicates that the market for this kind of community is huge!

Noah: Very interesting! And, um, let me ask you: about how old are most of your residents?

Rosa: Oh, it varies, but we're mainly talking about people 55 years and older.

Eric: Yes, you know, the older generation is really different these days. My grandparents, for instance, love doing things. They both like to golf, and my grandfather manages to play tennis at least twice a week.

Noah: That's wonderful. And what kind of housing do you offer at Sun Village?

Rosa: Oh, we offer single-family homes, and then of course we have condominiums. There are over 22 plans to choose from!

Eric: Yeah, well, you know, a huge percent of people actually prefer living in their own homes. They just don't want the responsibility of taking care of all the outdoor work and repairs.

Noah: Well, I know that my parents refuse to sell their house anytime soon. OK, so, I'm assuming Sun Village also offers some kind of community facilities?

Eric: Oh, absolutely! I mean, the property is enormous – over 800 acres. And we have a state-of-the-art fitness facility and four golf courses.

Noah: Four?

Eric: Yep, four.

Noah: Wow, that's amazing. Sorry, go on.

Eric: Well, we want to ensure that people can remain active. I mean, too often if a gym or pool is crowded or hard to get to, people just give up and never go.

Rosa: I agree. I know I won't go to the gym at the end of the day anymore – between about 6 and 8 – because it's just too busy.

Eric: Right. And we also offer lots of cultural events at Sun Village. Everyone loves our cultural offerings. We have plays and concerts almost every week. And we have art shows at least once a month.

Noah: I'm sure they're a big hit with the residents. Well, our time's about up here. I'd like to thank Rosa and Eric for being with us today. I know that I, for one, cannot wait for retirement! I'm going to devote my time to learning Chinese and bird-watching and …

🔊 8.2

1 What do you mean by the term "active adult community"?

2 So, at Sun Village we want to attract people who can live on their own.

3 Oh, we offer single-family homes, and then of course we have condominiums.

4 Wow, that's amazing! Sorry, go on.

5 I mean, too often if a gym or pool is crowded or hard to get to, people just give up and never go.

6 I know I won't go to the gym at the end of the day anymore.

CREDITS

The authors and publishers acknowledge the following sources of copyright material and are grateful for the permissions granted. While every effort has been made, it has not always been possible to identify the sources of all the material used, or to trace all copyright holders. If any omissions are brought to our notice, we will be happy to include the appropriate acknowledgements on reprinting and in the next update to the digital edition, as applicable.

Photo credits
Front cover photographs by (woman) IZO/Shutterstock and (street) f11photo/Shutterstock.

Corpus
Development of this publication has made use of the Cambridge English Corpus (CEC). The CEC is a multi-billion word computer database of contemporary spoken and written English. It includes British English, American English, and other varieties of English. It also includes the Cambridge Learner Corpus, developed in collaboration with the University of Cambridge ESOL Examinations. Cambridge University Press has built up the CEC to provide evidence about language use that helps to produce better language teaching materials.

Cambridge Dictionaries
Cambridge dictionaries are the world's most widely used dictionaries for learners of English. The dictionaries are available in print and online at dictionary.cambridge.org. Copyright © Cambridge University Press, reproduced with permission.

Typeset by emc design ltd

Audio production by CityVox New York